OSPREY AIRCRAFT OF THE ACES® • 36

P-39 Airacobra Aces of World War 2

SERIES EDITOR: TONY HOLMES

OSPREY AIRCRAFT OF THE ACES® • 36

P-39 Airacobra Aces of World War 2

George Mellinger and John Stanaway

OSPREY
AVIATION

Front cover
At 0810 hrs on 1 May 1942, the 8th Fighter Group's 36th Fighter Squadron scrambled five Airacobras from Seven-Mile strip, located near Port Moresby, New Guinea. Flown by Lts Erickson, Campbell (of the 35th FS), Hooker, Armstrong and Don 'Fibber' McGee, these aircraft had been sent aloft after Allied spotters had radioed the airfield warning of approaching enemy aircraft. However, once airborne, the American pilots failed to find any trace of Japanese aerial activity. After patrolling the skies north of Port Moresby for almost an hour, McGee realised that his fuel was nearing exhaustion. Plotting a course for home, he had just turned towards Seven-Mile strip when he sighted Zeros over the mist-shrouded airfield. Despite the low fuel state of his P-39D (41-6941), McGee decided to attack, and making full use of his superior altitude, he quickly despatched one of the Japanese fighters. The remaining Zero pilots did their utmost to avenge their fallen comrade, McGee's Airacobra having its tail holed by cannon shells and a wing punctured by machine gun rounds. Struggling back to base in his battle-weary fighter, McGee also found a bullet hole in the canopy perspex above his head when he extricated himself from the cockpit after landing. The wreckage of his Zero was located about a mile from the airstrip, 'Fibber' McGee's victory being the first of 94 confirmed kills credited to the 36th FS during the course of World War 2
(*cover artwork by Iain Wyllie*)

Title page photograph
Two war-weary P-39Q-1s of the 318th FG sit quietly at dispersal at an airfield on Oahu, Hawaii, in late 1943. These aircraft were amongst a handful of veteran Airacobras and Warhawks issued to the group's three fighter squadrons following their activation in Hawaii in mid-October 1942. Both fighters carry mission markers and door art, the Airacobra in the foreground (42-19549) being christened *TARAWA BOOM DEAY* and the aircraft behind it *MY GAL SAL IV* (*via Michael O'Leary*)

First published in Great Britain in 2001 by Osprey Publishing, Elms Court, Chapel Way, Botley, Oxford, OX2 9LP
E-mail: info@ospreypublishing.com

© 2001 Osprey Publishing Limited

ISBN 1 84176 204 0

Edited by Tony Holmes
Page design by TT Designs, T & B Truscott
Cover Artwork by Iain Wyllie
Aircraft Profiles by Jim Laurier
Scale Drawings by Mark Styling
Index by Alan Thatcher
Origination by Grasmere Digital Imaging, Leeds, UK
Printed through Bookbuilders, Hong Kong

01 02 03 04 05   10 9 8 7 6 5 4 3 2 1

EDITOR'S NOTE
To make this best-selling series as authoritative as possible, the Editor would be interested in hearing from any individual who may have relevant photographs, documentation or first-hand experiences relating to the elite fighter pilots, and their aircraft, of the various theatres of war. Any material used will be credited to its original source. Please write to Tony Holmes at 10 Prospect Road, Sevenoaks, Kent, TN13 3UA, Great Britain, or by e-mail at: tony.holmes@osprey-jets.freeserve.co.uk

ACKNOWLEDGEMENTS
Thank you to the former P-39 pilots who provided useful material, namely Clarence E 'Bud' Anderson, Hugh Dow, Roger Ames, Paul Bechtel, Charles King, Stanley Andrews and Douglas Canning. Fellow aviation historians Rhodes Arnold, Steve Blake, Jack Cook, Carl Molesworth, Michael O'Leary, Jerry Scutts, Dwayne Tabatt and Bill Wolf also made significant contributions.

Back cover photograph
Col Aleksandr Pokryshkin (at the wheel of a lend-lease Willys Jeep) and two of his pilots are seen inspecting a recently-captured German airfield in the early spring of 1945. Behind them is the wreckage of a still smouldering Fw 189 *Rama* observation aircraft (*via Petrov*)

For a catalogue of all Osprey Publishing titles please contact us at:

Osprey Direct UK, PO Box 140, Wellingborough, Northants NN8 4ZA, UK
E-mail: info@ospreydirect.co.uk

Osprey Direct USA, c/o Motorbooks International, 729 Prospect Ave, PO Box 1, Osceola, WI 54020, USA
E-mail: info@ospreydirectusa.com

Or visit our website: www.ospreypublishing.com

CONTENTS

INT ODUCTION

Brigadier-General Charles 'Chuck' Yeager of breaking the sound barrier fame stated in his autobiography, 'I had about 500 hours in the P-39, and thought it was about the best airplane I ever flew.' This statement may show more of Yeager's exuberance than other historical evidence, but he also made the claim that pilot ability had more to do with aerial victories than the relative merit of various fighter types. So it is with the P-39. The Bell fighter had some sterling qualities, but most other single-engined fighters had insurmountable advantages – especially above 12,000 ft.

Perhaps the most significant contribution made by the P-39 to American World War 2 air power was that it gave a number of future aces their first experience of flying a fighter. Highly successful pilots such as John Meyer (24 aerial kills in Europe) and Tom Lynch (20 kills in the Southwest Pacific) first flew combat missions with the P-39. Several others even managed to gain a small number of confirmed claims in the Pacific and Mediterranean theatres with the Bell fighter. However, the USAAF's general lack of confidence in the fighter often relegated the Airacobra to secondary duties such as convoy patrol or local transport aircraft escort.

The first serious blow to the prestige of the P-39 was its rejection by the Royal Air Force. Only one RAF

This P-39C belongs to the 31st Pursuit Group, which was activated with the Airacobra on 1 February 1940. This particular model had an arrangement of four 0.30-in machine guns clustered around the cannon in the nose – when a pair of 0.50-in guns was later fitted in the nose, the smaller calibre weapons were moved to the wings. The USAAF was never entirely satisfied with the armament fitted to the P-39/P-400, and this original layout would have significantly reduced the kill rate attained by Airacobra pilots in the first months of the war in the Pacific

In this classic pre-war photograph (almost certainly taken in 1940), an early-build P-39C formates with a YP-43 Lancer (forerunner of Republic's P-47), a series production P-40B and a pre-production YP-38 (*Michael O'Leary*)

This line-up shot of 40th PS/31st PG P-39Ds was taken at Selfridge Field, Michigan, at around the time of the Carolina Maneuvers of late 1941 (*via Michael O'Leary*)

A young second lieutenant admires the artwork applied to the door of his P-39D-1. All the aircraft assigned to the 40th PS pre-war were decorated with the unit's stylish 'Red Devils' badge, inspired by the outfit's nickname. The 40th FS went to war with the 35th FG in New Guinea in the spring of 1942 (*via Michael O'Leary*)

Bursting with pride, future triple ace Lt Clarence 'Bud' Anderson strikes a pose prior to entering the cockpit of his P-39Q-10 42-20746 in October 1943. The aircraft features the blood-thirsty (and unofficial) emblem of the 363rd FS on its cockpit door, this unit being assigned to the newly-formed 357th FG at Oroville, in California (*via 'Bud' Anderson*)

unit (No 601 Sqn) flew any operational sorties with the type, and the judgement of the British pilots was largely negative. Most of the aircraft in the batch that was scheduled for the RAF were sent to Australia, where they were used in combat under the designation P-400. In their first air battles during the middle of 1942 the P-39s enjoyed mixed success, losing many of their number, but helping keep the Japanese air offensive against New Guinea and Guadalcanal off-balance until the Allies took the initiative late in the year. However, some of the criticism from USAAF pilots was quite severe, reinforcing the decision to replace the type.

Opinion was just the reverse with lend-lease P-39s sent to the USSR. After the disappointing initial engagements between Soviet fighters such as the I-16 and MiG-3 and the Luftwaffe's Messerschmitt Bf 109s, anything would seem to have been an improvement. However, several types of Allied fighter were viewed with indifference by the Russians, with such stalwarts as the Hawker Hurricane and Curtiss P-40 being met with indifference, while the P-39 was highly regarded.

At low altitude the Airacobra could display sparkling performance, causing problems for Luftwaffe pilots and terror for troops on the ground. The Russian philosophy of air power was tactical in nature, with fighters and bombers being employed as 'flying artillery pieces' against enemy troops and equipment. Many of the leading Russian aces scored most, or all, of their victories with the P-39 – by an informal count, more than 30 Russian Airacobra pilots scored at least 20 victories in the type.

Thus, the P-39 had a decidedly mixed career. Most of the American pilots that flew it were glad to get into newer types, but nearly all of them

'Bud' Anderson's first *OLD CROW* (note the nickname just above the fighter's nose gear) sits on the frontline at Oroville. Like most pilots that flew the P-39, Anderson had a healthy respect for the fighter's handling qualities. 'The P-39 could be tricky. "It'll tumble and spin, and soon auger in", as one of our drinking songs aptly put. It had a reputation for tumbling end over end, which hardly inspired its pilots' (*via 'Bud' Anderson*)

'Bud' Anderson is joined by his crew chief, Otto Heino (centre), and an unnamed armourer on the flightline at Oroville in the autumn of 1943 (*via 'Bud' Anderson*)

Originally delivered to the RAF as Airacobra I BX187, this aircraft was one of 179 Bell fighters taken back by the USAAF in Britain in late 1942 following their rejection for frontline service by the customer. Redesignated P-400s, the vast majority of these fighters had remained in crates at the Eighth Air Force's aircraft depot at Burtonwood, in Lancashire, following their arrival in England the previous year. They were duly assembled and prepared for service in North Africa with Twelfth Air Force units. Deemed fully operational, and fitted with an external fuel tank, this P-39 is ready for its long ferry flight (*via Michael O'Leary*)

remembered the flying characteristics of the P-39 with affection. The Russians were overtly fond of the Bell fighter, creating some remarkable records for the machine. Fewer aerial encounters were registered in the Pacific or Mediterranean, but within limits, the P-39 gave a reasonably good account of itself, scoring more than 300 victories with American forces, and considerably more with Soviet VVS fighter regiments.

P-39s IN THE SOUTH PACIFIC

During the early months of the Pacific war, while the Japanese enjoyed complete mastery of the air from China virtually to the shores of Australia itself, P-39s of the USAAF's 8th PG (all pursuit groups were redesignated fighter groups in May 1942) were being loaded aboard transport ships on the west coast of America, bound for the frontline in eastern New Guinea. Off-loaded in Australia during the first week of March 1942, the aircraft had been quickly reassembled and sent to Brisbane, in Queensland. The following month, the first detachments of P-39s from the 35th and 36th PSs deployed north to the frontline at Port Moresby. Several pilots were lost in accidents prior to the group's arrival in New Guinea, thus introducing the 8th PG to the formidable weather conditions synonymous with the area.

Despite these early losses, the group had achieved operational readiness by the end of April thanks to the tutelage of several veteran Australian Kittyhawk pilots. Blessed with no shortage of youthful optimism, the Americans were keen to engage the enemy, and on the last day of the month the 8th PG sortied 13 P-39s on an offensive sweep of the airfields at Lae and Salamaua, on the north coast of New Guinea.

The Japanese were caught by surprise, and the Americans succeeded in making a single strafing run that accounted for a jetty with a fuel dump, a radio station, other supply dumps and three seaplanes found at anchor. Lae-based Zeros were scrambled in time to interfere with the withdrawal of the marauding P-39s, however, and a four-for-four exchange took place – three American pilots eventually returned to Port Moresby.

Three of the downed Zeros were credited to Lt Col Boyd D 'Buzz' Wagner, who was one the first US aces of the Pacific war. He had claimed five Japanese fighters over the Philippines in December 1941 whilst flying P-40Es with the 17th PS, before fleeing to Australia. With his unit wiped out, Wagner was posted to V Fighter Command (FC) HQ and tasked with building up an effective US fighter force for deployment to New Guinea. The two units assigned this task (35th and 36th PSs) were P-39/P-400-equipped, so Wagner became an advocate of the Bell fighter.

Lt Col Boyd D 'Buzz' Wagner was one of the army air corps' luminaries of the early Pacific war period. He was already an ace in P-40s when he led the first P-39 mission on 30 April 1942, during the course of which he claimed three Zero kills near Salamaua. Having survived an extended tour in the Pacific, Wagner returned to the USA in late 1942 and was killed in a flying accident on 29 November that same year when his P-40K crashed near Eglin Field, in Florida (*via Krane*)

9

Lt Walt Harvey, who was amongst the first group of P-39 pilots to survive the disastrous ferry flight from Australia to New Guinea in early April, scored a victory for the 36th FS when he probably destroyed a Zero on 14 May 1942 (*via Harvey*)

Lt Don 'Fibber' McGee poses with his groundcrew at Seven-Mile strip sometime after claiming his final P-39 kills on 29 May 1942. He is certain that he scored five aerial victories with the Airacobra, despite official USAF records crediting him with just three confirmed kills and one probable victory (*via Cook*)

Seizing his chance to add to his tally of kills, Wagner led the 13-strong force on the Friday, 30 April, strafing mission. The P-39Ds flew some 180 miles north into the heart of enemy territory to reach their target, the formation leader later reporting;

'Our approach was made on Lae from 50 miles out to sea at an altitude of about 100 ft in order to prevent our detection. When about 20 miles out, four aeroplanes were sent ahead to engage the Japanese Security patrol over Lae Drome. The top cover drew the enemy security patrol off to the east of Lae Drome, and no aerial resistance was encountered during our strafing attack. Inaccurate ground machine gun and ack-ack fire was observed. A line of 13 to 15 bombers were strafed from a sea approach in a 3-3 aeroplane element, the fighters in each element adopting an echelon right formation.

'Our strafing aeroplanes were then attacked from above by several Zero fighters. Belly tanks were dropped immediately and throttles opened. Our formation began to pull away from the Zeros when the last four P-39s turned to engage three of the enemy fighters in combat. In the meantime, more Zeros had appeared, and it is estimated that we were attacked by 12 to 13 altogether. The four P-39s were now hopelessly outnumbered, so I turned the entire formation back and a terrific fight ensued between 13 P-39s and an equal number of Zeros. This fight continued down the coast for about 30 miles and then back again.'

As previously noted, four Zeros were claimed shot down by the P-39 pilots, and the Americans lost four fighters – three pilots eventually made it back to Port Moresby on foot and the fourth was reportedly captured and executed by the Japanese. Wagner's haul of three Zeros boosted his score to eight, making him the ranking US ace in-theatre at the time. The remaining Zero was credited to Maj George Greene, commander of the 35th PS.

The month of May 1942 was a decisive one in the defence of New Guinea, and the northern coast of Australia. Early in the month the Australia-bound invasion fleet was turned back during the Battle of the Coral Sea, while P-39s accounted for nearly 20 enemy aircraft during the ongoing defence of Port Moresby – 12 pilots were lost in return.

Several individuals who later became aces in other types of fighter scored their first kills in P-39s or P-400s in 1942. One such pilot was Don McGee, who claimed the 36th FS's first victory whilst patrolling over Port Moresby's Seven-Mile strip on 1 May. He spotted a Zero strafing his airstrip below, and he immediately gave chase.

Frustrated that he had missed the action over Lae and Salamaua the day before, McGee dived down on his unwitting opponent. Unfamiliar with the new gunsight recently installed in his P-39D (41-6941),

McGee consequently missed his target with his first bursts. However, the Zero pilot was either unaware or openly disdainful of the P-39 on his tail, and he let the American draw in close enough to make effective use of his gunsight. Firing a second telling burst at the fighter, McGee watched excitedly as the smoking Zero crashed into the jungle north of the airfield – later, he and some of his comrades found the wreckage about a mile north of the runway.

Despite four other pilots being airborne with 'Fibber' McGee on this 1 May mission, they could not prevent him being set upon by other Zeros in the area. Just escaping with his life, McGee succeeded in landing a badly shot up 41-6941 back at base. He was quickly informed by excited groundcrewmen of the extensive battle damage inflicted on his machine, and as he looked around in the cockpit, McGee saw a bullet hole in the rear canopy, and then felt a shattered pair of sunglasses that had been resting on his head during the pursuit! His P-39 had been so badly shot up that it was soon reduced to component parts, which were joined with sections from another damaged Airacobra to form an entirely new aeroplane.

McGee claimed a Zero probably destroyed four days later, and then on 29 May was credited with the destruction of two Mitsubishi fighters south-east of Port Moresby. Enjoying a rare altitude advantage during this engagement, he had used his superior height to bounce a large formation of Zeros. Future five-kill ace Lt Clifton Troxell also got a Zero on this day, the 35th FS pilot having claimed his first victory three days earlier (and a probable kill on 27 May).

Other future aces within the 8th FG to claim Zeros destroyed during this period included the 36th FS's Grover Gholson and the 80th FS's

Don McGee's P-39D-1 42-38338 *Nip's Nemesis II* was highly unusual in that it carried identical artwork and kill tallies on both sides of the fuselage – groundcrews were usually hard-pressed to find the time to decorate one side of an operational aeroplane, let alone both of them! The artwork on the doors of this machine show a Japanese fighter being grabbed by a God-like hand. 'Fibber' McGee would claim a further two kills flying P-38s with the 80th FS during the course of 1943, before going on to score his final victory in a P-51D over Germany whilst commanding the 357th FG's 363rd FS in March 1945 (*via Cook*)

Lt Clifton Troxell is helped into his P-39F, nicknamed *UNCLE DUD*, by his crew chief, Pete Gino, towards the the end of 1942. Serving with the 35th FS at the time, Troxell claimed two confirmed victories and a probable with the P-39 in late May 1942. He would score two more kills in a P-38G on 15 September 1943 and a solitary victory with a P-40N on Boxing Day of that same year to qualify as an ace (*via Gino*)

Lts Walt Harvey and Grover Gholson
(first and second on the left) pose
with comrades from the 36th FS in
New Guinea. Having claimed a
solitary kill with the P-39, Gholson
would score four more victories
with the P-38H in 1943 after being
transferred into the crack 475th FG's
432nd FS (*via Gholson*)

The intricately detailed door art
carried on Maj Joe McNay's P-39 in
mid-1942 featured a helmeted
'Donald Duck', his three nephews
and a rather bent Airacobra! The
major took command of the 36th FS
in the midst of the May fighting, and
led the unit through one of its most
difficult periods of action. McNay
remained in command until
November of that year

Lt Tom Lynch leans out of the
cockpit of his 39th PS/31st PG P-39D
41-6733 between sorties in the USA
in late 1941. The artwork on the
entry door depicts a 'flying cobra',
inspired by the unit's nickname. The
39th transferred to the 35th PG in
February 1942, and deployed to
Australia, and onward to New
Guinea, soon afterwards. Although
having trained on the latest
Airacobras to reach the army air
corps back in America, the 39th PS
had to make do with technically
inferior P-400s once in the frontline,
as they were all that was available
at the time (*via Krane*)

Danny Roberts. Both pilots would
finish their scoring when they were
transferred to the crack P-38-
equipped 475th FG.

Gholson claimed a Zero on 14
May over Port Moresby, and nearly
put paid to his own career while
attacking a second enemy fighter 15
days later. Having scrambled to
intercept a large force of Zeros, his
section then spotted a second group
of fighters just as they were about to
'bounce' a trailing flight of P-39s
some distance below them. Gholson
followed his leader down into the
fight, hitting a Zero in the wings with several well aimed bursts.

The Japanese pilot threw his agile Zero into a climbing turn, but the
relentless Gholson followed him until his P-39 fell away in a wild spin,
straight into the midst of the whirling dogfight below. The American later
stated that he never again felt so helpless in combat as when he was trying
to recover from the spin amidst numerous Zeros that were lining up on his
tail! Just as he regained control of the P-39, he was surrounded by tracers,
and he heard the automatic 'chug'
and 'ping' of cannon shells and
machine guns being fired from the
Zeros sat close behind him.

Wounded by enemy fire,
Gholson realised that his only
chance of survival lay in him hastily
abandoning his badly damaged
fighter, so he bailed out. Having
survived this ordeal, he linked up
with local tribesman, who guided
him to a plantation, where he spent
two weeks recovering from thirst,
hunger and a raging fever.

One of the USAAF's highest-scoring aces in the Pacific also claimed his first kills in the Airacobra during May 1942. Lt Tom Lynch was one of a handful of 39th FS pilots temporarily assigned to the 8th FG to gain battle experience at Port Moresby prior to their own group (the 35th FG) being thrown into action. Flying a 35th FS P-400, he claimed two Zeros probably destroyed on the morning of 20 May over Waigani, and these were later confirmed as destroyed by an Australian army patrol that discovered the wreckage of two Zeros in the area.

Six days later Lynch was part of a flight of 35th FS machines that was escorting five transports bound for the frontline base at Wau. En route, the formation was intercepted by 16 Zeros, which enjoyed a height advantage of an additional 3000 ft. Undeterred, Lynch immediately turned his P-400 into the approaching Zeros, and he and Lt Gene Wahl each claimed a fighter shot down. Thanks to their tenacious defending, all five transports landed safely.

When the 39th FS officially commenced operations at the beginning of June, its pilots were eager, if innocent, in the ways of fighting a dangerous and combat-seasoned enemy. One of the first pilots to feel the full force

This photograph of Lt Curran 'Jack' Jones was taken at about the time he downed the Zero reportedly flown by 15-kill ace Satoshi Yoshino of the Tainan *Kokutai*. Note the future ace's non-regulation footwear! Jones would destroy a further four Japanese fighters in the first three months of 1943, by which time the 39th FS had re-equipped with the P-38F (*via Jones*)

of the Zero was Gene Wahl, who was forced down south of Rigo during the unit's opening engagement on 9 June. He wandered through the typically rugged wilderness that surrounded Port Moresby until he was returned to base battered and bandaged, but still full of fight, six days later. On the same day, Lts Lynch and Adkins rejoined the unit following a spell in hospital with Dengue Fever.

Returning to 9 June, future 39th FS ace Lt Curran 'Jack' Jones avenged the temporary loss of squadronmate Gene Wahl when he claimed a Zero destroyed whilst flying a P-400. His flight had been sent into action to help defend a squadron of B-26s that had come under attack as they headed home after bombing Lae. Jones managed to get on the tail of a Zero that was attacking the rest of his flight, and he quickly disabled the enemy fighter. The Japanese pilot climbed out onto the wing of his doomed Zero, pausing long enough for Jones to spot the forlorn look on the face of his victim. Years after the war it was learned that the probable identity of the Zero pilot was 15-victory ace Satoshi Yoshino.

Top right
Lt John L Jones of the 80th FS stands beside P-39D-2 41-38553, which had previously served with the 35th FS. When the 80th first entered combat in July 1942, many of its P-39s and P-400s were combat-weary veterans that had already seen much action with recently relieved squadrons – *Papuan Panic!* was one such machine. The 80th FS had trained in northern Australia in preparation for its first deployment to New Guinea in July 1942, and the unit enjoyed only modest success in action until it converted to P-38s in February 1943 (*via Krane*)

Two sharkmouthed Airacobras of the 80th FS taxy out at the start of a mission in late 1942. The location of this rudimentary airstrip remains unrecorded, although it is almost certainly one of the numerous airfields (possibly Turnbull) that surrounded Port Moresby (*via Krane*)

Despite these isolated successes, the P-39 pilots were finding it difficult to defeat the well-flown Zeros encountered in-theatre at this early stage of the war. This was brought home to the 39th FS on 16 June. The unit scrambled 18 fighters into the low overcast that blanketed the area when enemy aircraft were spotted heading for the airfields that surrounded Port Moresby. Two of the Airacobras were immediately forced to land with mechanical trouble, and the remaining sixteen pilots found themselves scattered above and below the clouds. The Zero pilots took full advantage of this confusion to bounce the Americans, and one P-39 was shot down and several others damaged.

Tom Lynch was one of those pilots scrambled on the 16th, and whilst trying to join up with other American fighters over Rigo, his lone fighter was 'bounced' by a pair of Zeros. Having escaped their attention, Lynch's P-39 was then set upon by four more Japanese fighters, who inflicted further damage to his machine. Flying for his life, the future ace used every trick he knew to escape, and he eventually shook off his pursuers. He then attempted to make it back to Seven-Mile strip, but before he could land the P-39's engine exploded, forcing Lynch to parachute into the bay off Port Moresby from a height of 800 ft. Fortunately for him he was wearing one of the life vests that had only recently arrived on the squadron.

Later, when fellow 39th FS pilots asked him how well the vest had worked, Lynch informed them that he had discarded it so as to facilitate his swimming through the shark-infested waters! As it happened, he was

Lt Ben Brown saw action in defence of Port Moresby with the 80th FS during mid-1942. Like many of his contemporaries, he was not a great fan of the Airacobra. 'The P-39 was a lot of fun to fly if you did not have to worry about somebody shooting at you or, conversely, if you had to try to shoot at somebody. It was a nice looking aeroplane, but on final summation, it was a bad aeroplane – a dog that could not do the job for which it was designed' (*via Michael O'Leary*)

rescued by a tribesman in a boat. Tom Lynch had suffered a broken right arm whilst bailing out, and this kept him out of combat for many weeks.

By the end of July, when the 39th FS's surviving pilots were pulled out of the frontline for a rest, their initial enthusiasm for action had been worn down by the conditions they faced in New Guinea. Many of them had had to endure mechanical maladies with the P-39, whilst at the same time attempting to counter ferocious attacks perpetrated by an enemy whose devotion to duty was now legendary. To further compound their problems, most of the pilots were suffering from the effects of malaria or Dengue Fever, which sapped even the high spirits of young P-39 pilots.

Other P-39-equipped units replaced the 39th FS in New Guinea during the latter half of July, although the unit got in one 'last lick' when a flight of Airacobras (led by Frank Royal) strafed the Japanese landings at Gona. Having trouble keeping up with his squadronmates, Lt Ralph Martin came across a reconnaissance floatplane just as it was taking off near the invasion beach. Diving on the vulnerable machine, his guns failed on his first attack, so he came in for another pass, and this time he succeeded in shooting the aircraft down. Martin's kill was confirmed by Allied troops in the area, and this became the 39th FS's final P-39 victory of the war. Within two days of this success, the 80th FS had replaced the 39th FS in-theatre, the former unit inheriting some of its Airacobras.

Amongst the new crop of pilots to arrive at Port Moresby with the 80th FS was future 14-kill ace Lt Danny Roberts. He had talked himself out of an assignment to a unit based in a remote corner of the Australian outback and into the embryonic 80th FS. Grasping the opportunity with both hands, Roberts participated in one of the few aerial engagements that the squadron would experience with the P-39.

On the morning of 26 August, a flight of P-400s was patrolling over

Below
Airacobra I BW102 was one of nearly 200 British-ordered Bell fighters requisitioned by the US government following the Pearl Harbor raid in December 1941. Although similar to the P-39D, they were not identical, for the Airacobra I had a 20 mm Hispano cannon in the nose in place of the 37 mm weapon fitted to the D-model, as well as four 0.303-in machine guns rather than 0.30-in weapons. Other detail changes included 12-stack fish tail exhaust stacks, perspex door windows, no IFF set behind the pilot and a V-1710-35 (E4) engine fitted with automatic boost. Redesignated the P-400, the aircraft also boasted standard RAF early war day fighter Dark Earth and Dark Green camouflage. Hastily issued to units in the Southwest Pacific in 1942, they saw much service through to the end of the year. Nicknamed *THE FLAMING ARROW*, BW102 was the personal mount of the 39th FS's Lt Curran 'Jack' Jones. He claimed a single kill (a Zero reportedly flown by 15-kill ace Satoshi Yoshino of the Tainan *Kokutai*) with the Airacobra on 9 June, although official documentation fails to record whether he was flying this machine at the time (*via Michael O'Leary*)

The 41st FS's radio section get together for a group shot in late 1942. The 35th FG's three units (the 39th, 40th and 41st) relieved the 8th FG in June (*via Krane*)

Lt Charles King's P-400 BW176 is seen soon after it was turned over to the 80th FS at the end of July 1942. Its new owners decorated the fighter with a sharksmouth on the nose, and gave it a further identification marking in the form of a single letter below the cockpit. 80th FS records indicate that this P-400 remained operational until January 1943 (*via Hickey*)

Lt Col Boyd D 'Buzz' Wagner (right) poses with an armed enlisted man alongside an ex-39th FS P-39D in mid-1942. Despite already being an ace, Wagner's exploits in the Philippines in December 1941 were initially viewed with some scepticism by 8th FG pilots when he arrived in New Guinea. He quickly dispelled any disquiet by leading the first P-39 mission against Lae and Salamaua on 30 April 1942 (*via Hickey*)

Buna when they spotted a number of 2nd *Kokutai* Zeros in the process of taking off from a nearby airstrip. Roberts immediately dived on the hapless Japanese fighters, badly damaged one of them in his first pass. His attack was followed up by the remaining P-400s in his flight, which downed two Zeros that had just cleared the runway. Roberts and his wingman then turned into the surviving Zeros that had succeeded in getting airborne, and the future ace destroyed two more navy fighters.

After the battle had ended, the Americans claimed six Zeros shot down and a further three damaged. The Japanese declared that three of their 2nd *Kokutai* pilots had been killed, and a fourth had crash-landed his Zero, which was duly written off.

EVALUATIONS OF THE P-39

The first USAAF combat evaluation of the P-39 was made by Lt Col Boyd 'Buzz' Wagner within days of his initial contact with Japanese Zeros. Some of the ace's comments are surprising in light of the numerous negative opinions later expressed by American pilots that flew the Bell fighter in combat;

'The Zero outperformed the P-39 very markedly in manoeuvrability and climb. However, a P-39 without a belly tank could pull away from the Zero. The Zero had used several differences in construction and performance than those heretofore observed. A larger engine cowling was very evident, indicating the possibility of a higher-powered engine. This was further borne out because the Zero was able to keep up with the P-39 to an indicated speed of about 290 mph. At 325 mph indicated just above the water, the P-39 pulled slowly away out of range.

'In acceleration, the Zero was markedly better than the P-39, attaining a high speed from cruising in a very few seconds, while the P-39 was much slower. As a result, from a cruising start, the Zero could actually pull ahead of the P-39 for a few seconds and then the P-39 slowly drew away at full throttle and high RPM.

'Generally speaking, the P-39 is an excellent anti-bombardment fighter at altitudes up to 18,000 ft. Above 18,000 ft, performance is sluggish and rate of climb very low. The 37 mm cannon is an extremely desirable weapon, but "bugs" are still being eliminated. Stoppages in the air are frequent, and it is difficult to reload and recharge during combat because of the high loading and charging forces. Its effect against enemy aircraft (in the initial engagements) was excellent.

'Comparatively speaking, in performance the P-39 is believed to be about ten per cent better in every respect than the P-40, except in manoeuvrability, in which case the P-40 is slightly better.'

Wagner noted eight areas of criticism that probably presaged the rejection of the P-39 in the Pacific. These included lack of armour for the liquid-cooled engine, hydraulic propellers that threw oil on the windscreen, frequent gun stoppages, generally weak landing gear, obsolete radio installation, short range and poor performance above 18,000 ft.

Another Fifth Air Force ace who noted down his opinions of the P-39 was Charles King of the 39th FS. He was involved in a particularly rough engagement on 4 July, which saw three of his squadronmates shot down (all would eventually return) for claims of one Zero destroyed and four others damaged. King noticed a flight of Zeros below him during the battle, and he half-rolled to get on the tail of one of them, which easily shook him off after he had got in some good bursts (King failed to lodge any claims with the P-39).

The cockpit of a standard P-39D. The Airacobra's cockpit was designed specifically for a 5 ft 8 in pilot who weighed 200 lb when equipped with his parachute and full flying gear. For larger pilots the cockpit was definitely on the cramped side, but the wind-down windows in the entry doors helped a little bit when the aircraft was on the ground. This unique window layout was one thing about the P-39 which really stuck in the memory of most pilots that flew it. 'Bud' Anderson remembers, 'You could taxy the thing while resting your elbows on the sill, like cruising the boulevard on a Saturday night' (*via Michael O'Leary*)

Future five-kill ace Lt Charles King of the 39th FS flew P-400 BW176 from Seven-Mile strip in 1942, the fighter being personalised with this unique door insignia inspired by its pilot's surname. King's first crack at the Japanese on 4 July resulted in him being credited with damaging a Zero. Despite scoring all of his kills in P-38s during the course of 1943, he never forgot the fighting qualities of the P-400 (*via King*)

Lts William 'Dodo' Brown and Charles Able enjoy a cigarette between sorties in the 80th FS's dispersal area at Twelve-Mile strip, Port Moresby in September 1942. Within days of this photograph being taken, the unit had deployed with the rest of the 8th FG to the Milne Bay area, north-east of Port Moresby, to help defend the region from further Japanese encroachment along the eastern tip of New Guinea. All five of the P-400s visible in this shot boast sharksmouths and individual identification letters (*via Krane*)

Charles King only recently committed his thoughts to print in an effort to clarify some of the criticisms levelled at the P-39 over the years:

'The Bell P-39 (as well as the P-40) was not the type of aircraft to do battle with the Japanese fighters that we initially encountered in the Pacific. Wartime records are suspect, but there are many reasons to believe that the pilots flying these early fighters generally fought the Japanese to a draw, despite the fact that in the first months of the war the enemy pilots enjoyed a considerable advantage in terms of combat experience. The aeroplanes used by either side had both operational advantages and disadvantages. This resulted in a kill ratio that was realistically one-to-one. Because our fighters at this time were not good enough to give us a distinct

advantage over our foes, many of us – myself included – bad-mouthed the P-39. We all desperately wanted a fighter that would give us a longer life expectancy.

'Ironically, had the P-39 been equipped as originally proposed with a turbo supercharger, it would have been more than marginally superior to the Zero. This would have improved the fighter's altitude capability, which was sadly lacking, and which meant that we started most encounters at a disadvantage.

35th FS P-39D-1 41-38343 is seen just seconds after taking off from an airfield in the Milne Bay area at the end of 1942. Note how the pilot has already started to cycle away the aircraft's undercarriage

'The P-39's handling characteristics have also come in for some criticism too. However, I am convinced that the fighter did not "tumble", as has been widely reported. All tests to record a tumble were unsuccessful. It was easy to stall the aeroplane on its back, with a resultant flat inverted spin. In that situation, retarding the throttle would allow the aeroplane to drop into an easily recoverable normal spin. Loss of altitude in a flat spin was minimal, but to the disoriented pilot with a control stick that seemed useless, this was not apparent. The aeroplane oscillated slowly and horizontally as the nose dipped below the horizon and then rose above it. To some pilots this was interpreted as a tumble.

'As a junior officer I flew the Airacobra for a year before my squadron became one of the first to use the P-39/P-400 against the Japanese. In two months of combat I flew 25 sorties, and encountered the enemy on numerous occasions. In that period the unit (39th) tallied nine kills and had nine pilots shot down – all of them survived. Other early units suffered greater losses, but were also credited with more kills. My study of the records of the P-40 units indicates they had similar, if not better, records. The AVG in China and the 49th PG based at Darwin are good examples.'

Japanese views of the P-39 were understandably disdainful. Translations of Japanese recognition manuals reveal that the enemy considered most of the early American fighter types they encountered in China or the Southwest Pacific to be markedly inferior to the Zero. And those pilots who engaged the P-39 over New Guinea viewed the Bell fighter in much the same light. Oddly enough, the P-40 was held in even less regard, despite the Curtiss fighter being able to out dive the Zero in combat. Veteran P-40 pilots are sometimes puzzled by the Japanese indifference to their trusty Warhawks, which they used to good effect when creating a victory ratio of five enemy aircraft claimed for every P-40 lost.

The main drawbacks of the P-39, according to Japanese assessment, were its lack of manoeuvrability, relatively fragile construction and sluggish initial diving speed. For the most part, P-39s were at least equal in speed to the Zero near sea level, and could deliver an extremely lethal burst of fire – if all the guns worked at the same time.

LAST USAAF P-39 VICTORIES OF 1942

The last 8th FG aces to score victories in the P-39 made their claims at the end of 1942 whilst helping to defend Milne Bay. On 7 December – the

Future six-kill ace Joe McKeon scored a victory (in P-39D-1 41-38353) for the 35th FS when he claimed a Zero over Buna on 7 December 1942. During the same sortie fellow 8th FG pilot Lt George 'Wheaties' Welch downed two Zeros and two 'Vals' to add to his previous tally of four kills scored over Pearl Harbor exactly one year earlier (*via Dennis Cooper*)

Capt Rasmussen pauses on the wing of his P-39D-1 (41-38356) prior to strapping into the fighter. This photograph was taken during the Milne Bay defence at the end of 1942. His crew chief, Tony Trotta, is the middle figure of the three groundcrewmen (*via Trotta*)

first anniversary of the attack on Pearl Harbor – 15 P-39s of the 35th and 36th FSs engaged seven 'Val' dive-bombers, escorted by two Zeros. Amongst the American pilots airborne on this day was the 36th's Lt George 'Wheaties' Welch, flying P-39D-1 41-38359. Exactly one year earlier, he had downed four Japanese aircraft during the Pearl Harbor raid whilst at the controls of a P-40B of the 47th PS. Desperate to 'make ace', Welch finally got the chance over Milne Bay.

Spotting the Zeros as they strafed Buna, he made good use of his superior height to dive down at speed from 4000 ft straight onto the tail of a Japanese fighter. The Zero attempted to flee in the direction of Kokoda, but Welch quickly caught him up and sent the fighter down in flames – he had just become the 36th FS's first ace. Moments later Welch attacked a 'Val', which exploded after being hit by a five-second burst. He then saw another dive-bomber at low-level over the sea, and closed to within just a few yards prior to shooting the 'Val' down into the water. Future ace Joe McKeon also claimed a Zero to begin his victory tally, which continued with the 475th FG and finally ended in Europe with the 20th FG.

Yet another ace who would transfer from the 36th FS to the 475th also claimed a solitary P-39 kill during the course of December 1942. On the morning of the 28th, Lt Verl Jett was patrolling over Goodenough Island in P-39D-1 41-38396 when he encountered a Japanese reconnaissance aeroplane and duly shot it down. This action earned Jett a Silver Star, and within a year he was leading the 475th FG's 431st FS.

The Milne Bay period from October 1942 through to the end of the year proved once again that the Airacobra was a useful, if not entirely desirable, fighter type. Some of the comments made by pilots who had already traded in the P-39 for other types were occasionally abusive. Indeed, one such individual from the 39th FS suggested after his first engagement with Zeros that a truck would have made a better interceptor, because it would climb faster and was more manoeuvrable than the Bell fighter.

By the end of 1942 the P-39 units of V FC had claimed about 80 Japanese aircraft destroyed for a similar number of P-39s lost, and about 25 pilots killed or missing in action. By any standard, the P-39/P-400 had held its ground against a skilled and determined enemy that had been dominant in the Pacific throughout the first year of the war.

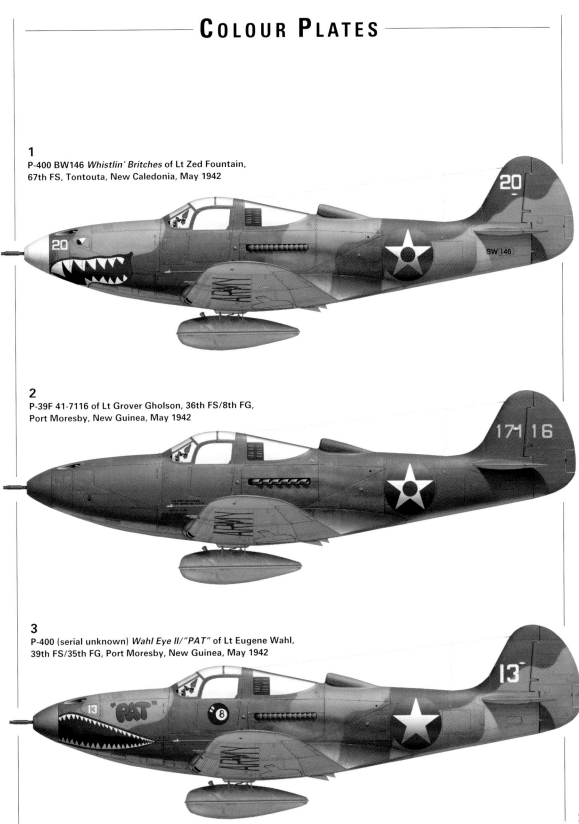

1
P-400 BW146 *Whistlin' Britches* of Lt Zed Fountain,
67th FS, Tontouta, New Caledonia, May 1942

2
P-39F 41-7116 of Lt Grover Gholson, 36th FS/8th FG,
Port Moresby, New Guinea, May 1942

3
P-400 (serial unknown) *Wahl Eye II/"PAT"* of Lt Eugene Wahl,
39th FS/35th FG, Port Moresby, New Guinea, May 1942

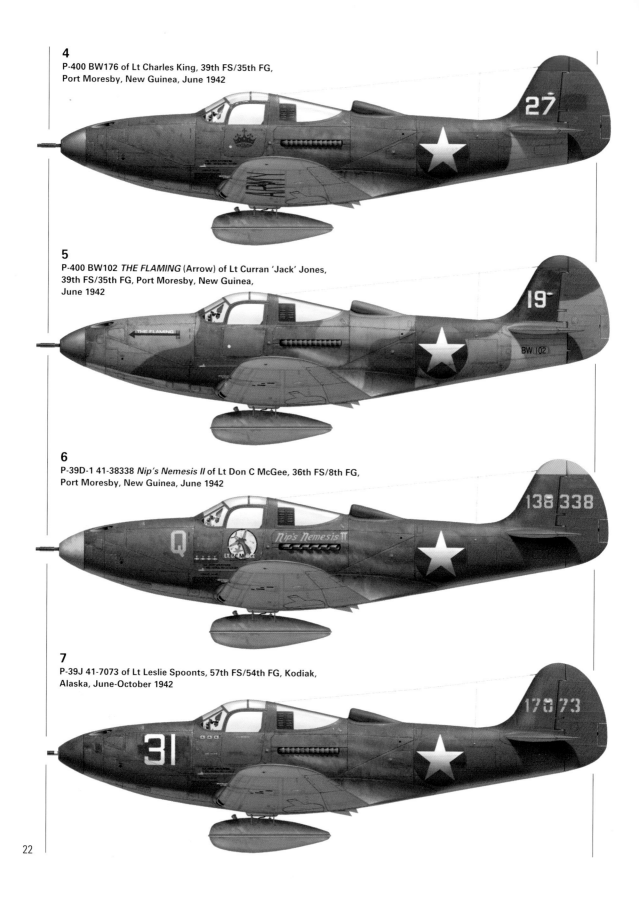

4
P-400 BW176 of Lt Charles King, 39th FS/35th FG,
Port Moresby, New Guinea, June 1942

5
P-400 BW102 *THE FLAMING* (Arrow) of Lt Curran 'Jack' Jones,
39th FS/35th FG, Port Moresby, New Guinea,
June 1942

6
P-39D-1 41-38338 *Nip's Nemesis II* of Lt Don C McGee, 36th FS/8th FG,
Port Moresby, New Guinea, June 1942

7
P-39J 41-7073 of Lt Leslie Spoonts, 57th FS/54th FG, Kodiak,
Alaska, June-October 1942

8
P-39D (serial unknown) of Lt Joseph McKeon, 35th FS/8th FG,
Milne Bay, New Guinea, November 1942

9
P-39D-1 41-36345 *Pelikia* of Lt George Welch, 36th FS/8th FG,
Milne Bay, New Guinea, November 1942

10
P-39D-1 41-38295 of Lt Gerald R Johnson,
57th FS/54th FG, Kodiak, Alaska, late 1942

11
P-39K-1 42-4358 of Lt William McDonough, 40th FS/35th FG,
Nadzab, New Guinea, February 1943

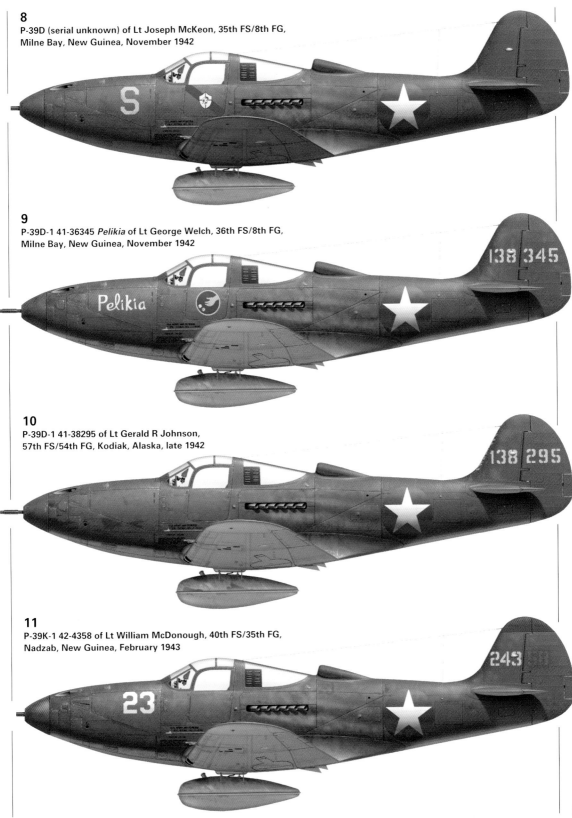

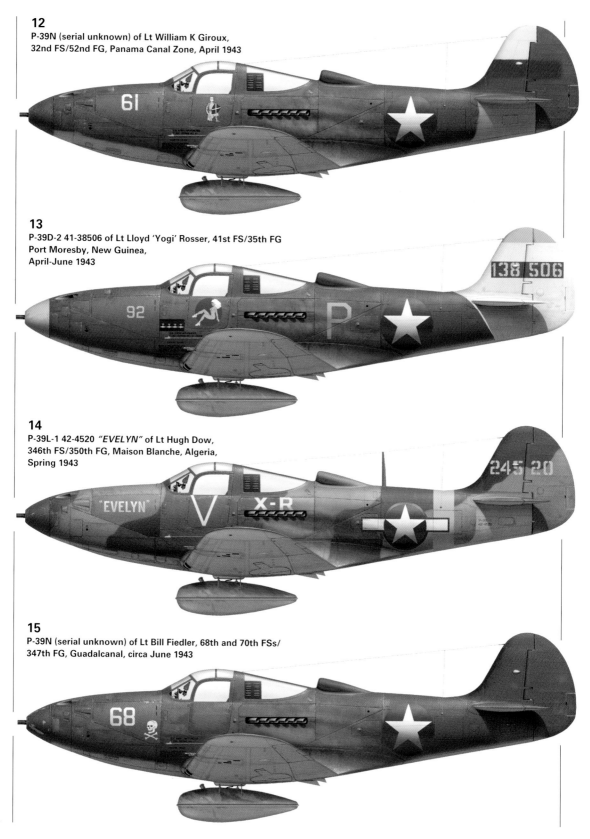

12
P-39N (serial unknown) of Lt William K Giroux,
32nd FS/52nd FG, Panama Canal Zone, April 1943

13
P-39D-2 41-38506 of Lt Lloyd 'Yogi' Rosser, 41st FS/35th FG
Port Moresby, New Guinea,
April-June 1943

14
P-39L-1 42-4520 *"EVELYN"* of Lt Hugh Dow,
346th FS/350th FG, Maison Blanche, Algeria,
Spring 1943

15
P-39N (serial unknown) of Lt Bill Fiedler, 68th and 70th FSs/
347th FG, Guadalcanal, circa June 1943

16
P-39 (unknown sub-type and serial) of Lt Bob Yaeger, 40th FS/35th FG,
Tsili-Tsili, New Guinea, August 1943

17
P-39 (unknown sub-type and serial) of Lt Tom Winburn,
40th FS/35th FG, Tsili-Tsili, New Guinea,
August 1943

18
P-39N-5 42-18805 *TODDY III* of Capt Hilbert,
41st FS/35th FG, Tsili-Tsili, New Guinea,
September 1943

19
P-39L-1 42-4687 *Little Toni*, flown by various pilots of the
362nd FS/357th FG, Hayward, California, September 1943

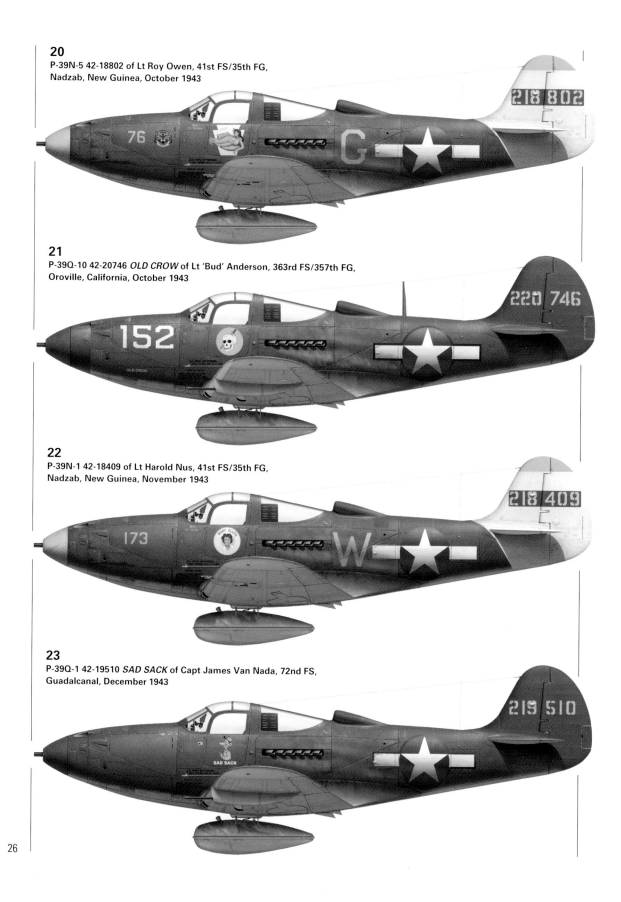

20
P-39N-5 42-18802 of Lt Roy Owen, 41st FS/35th FG,
Nadzab, New Guinea, October 1943

21
P-39Q-10 42-20746 *OLD CROW* of Lt 'Bud' Anderson, 363rd FS/357th FG,
Oroville, California, October 1943

22
P-39N-1 42-18409 of Lt Harold Nus, 41st FS/35th FG,
Nadzab, New Guinea, November 1943

23
P-39Q-1 42-19510 *SAD SACK* of Capt James Van Nada, 72nd FS,
Guadalcanal, December 1943

24
Airacobra I AH636 'White 33' of Capt Ivan Dmitrievich Gaidaenko,
19 GIAP, Autumn 1942

25
P-39D-2 41-38428 'White 37' of Capt Vadim Ivanovich Fadeev,
16 GIAP, April 1943

26
P-39K-1 42-4403 'White 21' of Snr Lt Dmitrii Borisovich Glinka,
45 IAP, Kuban, Spring 1943

27
P-39Q (serial unknown) 'White 10' of Capt Pavel Stepanovich
Kutakhov, 19 GIAP, Shongui, late 1943

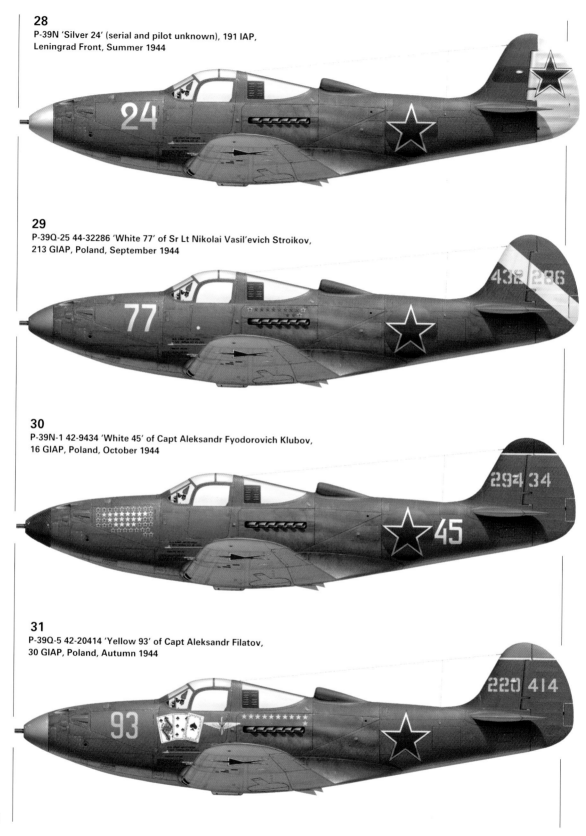

28
P-39N 'Silver 24' (serial and pilot unknown), 191 IAP,
Leningrad Front, Summer 1944

29
P-39Q-25 44-32286 'White 77' of Sr Lt Nikolai Vasil'evich Stroikov,
213 GIAP, Poland, September 1944

30
P-39N-1 42-9434 'White 45' of Capt Aleksandr Fyodorovich Klubov,
16 GIAP, Poland, October 1944

31
P-39Q-5 42-20414 'Yellow 93' of Capt Aleksandr Filatov,
30 GIAP, Poland, Autumn 1944

32
P-39N-0 42-9033 'White 01' (port view) of Capt Ivan Il'ich Babak,
100 GIAP, Germany, January 1945

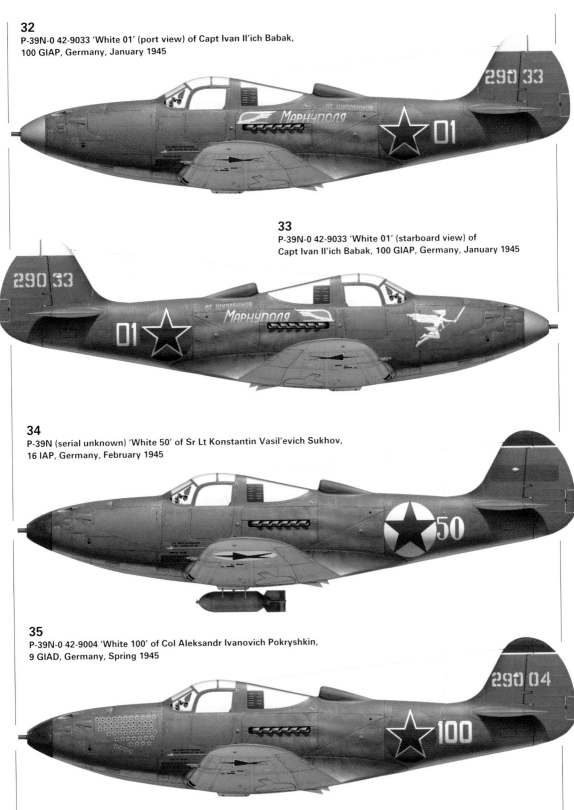

33
P-39N-0 42-9033 'White 01' (starboard view) of
Capt Ivan Il'ich Babak, 100 GIAP, Germany, January 1945

34
P-39N (serial unknown) 'White 50' of Sr Lt Konstantin Vasil'evich Sukhov,
16 IAP, Germany, February 1945

35
P-39N-0 42-9004 'White 100' of Col Aleksandr Ivanovich Pokryshkin,
9 GIAD, Germany, Spring 1945

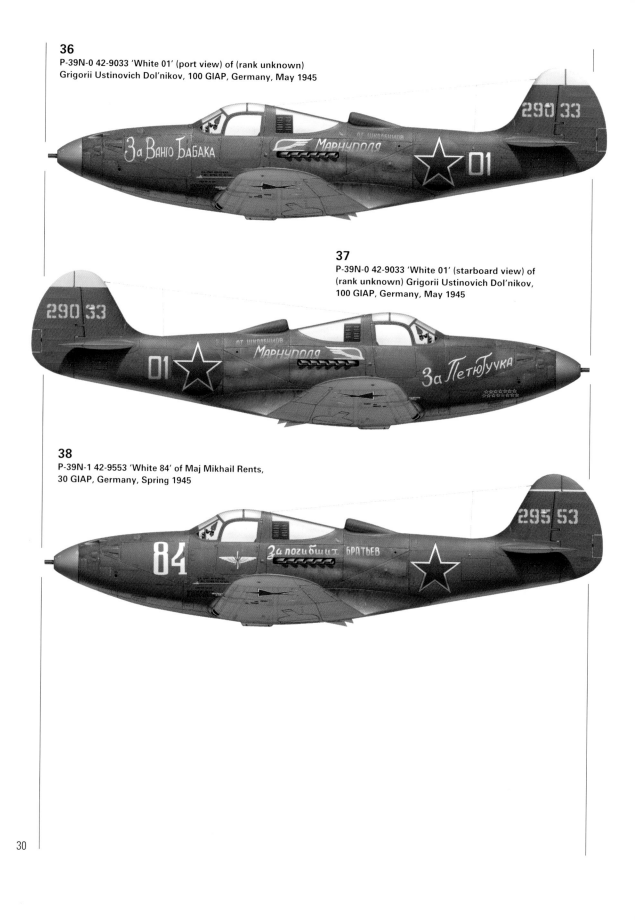

36
P-39N-0 42-9033 'White 01' (port view) of (rank unknown)
Grigorii Ustinovich Dol'nikov, 100 GIAP, Germany, May 1945

37
P-39N-0 42-9033 'White 01' (starboard view) of
(rank unknown) Grigorii Ustinovich Dol'nikov,
100 GIAP, Germany, May 1945

38
P-39N-1 42-9553 'White 84' of Maj Mikhail Rents,
30 GIAP, Germany, Spring 1945

THIrTEENTH AIR
FORCE SUCCESSES

Whilst P-39s and P-400s of the 8th and 35th FGs slugged it out with the Japanese over eastern New Guinea, Airacobra units destined for service with the Thirteenth Air Force in the South Pacific were working up in New Caledonia and on Christmas Island. The first five aircraft to go into action were P-400s of the 67th FS, which flew into Guadalcanal's Henderson Field on 22 August.

The flight's CO was Capt Dale Brannon, and he shared the unit's first kill with Lt Deltis Fincher just 48 hours after the P-400s had arrived on the embattled island. The flight had intercepted 'Val' dive-bombers heading for Henderson, and in the resulting melee, one of the escorting Zeros was shot down. Brannon was in the thick of the action again on 30 August, when he went to the rescue of some P-400s that were under attack. He swiftly shot down two Zeros, but could not prevent the loss of four Airacobras, and their pilots.

The Japanese threw everything they had at the American invaders on Guadalcanal during August and September, losing many aircraft to the US Navy and Marine fighters that rose to the island's defence. Victories came slowly to the P-400s, however, and no further claims were made until Capts John W Mitchell and William Shaw caught a pair of floatplanes that were protecting the withdrawal of ships which had landed reinforcements on Guadalcanal in the early hours of 9 October.

Downing one aircraft apiece, Mitchell added a Zero to his score two weeks later, followed by another floatplane (a 'Rufe') on 7 November. He later became an ace in the P-38, and led the celebrated long-range interception mission that claimed the life of Adm Isoruko Yamamoto.

Despite these sporadic successes, perplexing problems still attended operations flown by the P-400s, with perhaps the most troublesome being the unsatisfactory high-altitude performance of the fighter. Time after time pilots would take off on interception missions, only to find the enemy at too high an altitude (anything above 20,000 ft) for them to effect an intercept. The fighter's high-pressure oxygen system was not suited to high level combat, and neither was its Allison engine.

This 67th FS P-400 was nicknamed *Fancy Nancy*, the fighter carrying the titling above the 12-stack exhaust. It was photographed at Henderson Field, on Guadalcanal, soon after the first flight of five P-400s had flown in on 22 August 1942 (*via Bell Textron*)

Future 15-kill ace John Mitchell (right) is seen during a lull in the action at Henderson. Flying with the 70th FS during the unit's first spell on Guadalcanal, he scored three times with the P-39 (*via Ames*)

Forced to leave the high altitude fighting to other types, the Airacobra next tasted success on 3 December when a large Japanese troop convoy was intercepted by aircraft from Guadalcanal. SBD dive-bombers and TBF torpedo-bombers managed to damage at least one Japanese destroyer, whilst the fighter escorts claimed ten F1M 'Pete' observation floatplanes – four of these were credited to the P-400s of the 67th FS. One pilot credited with a kill was Lt Zed Fountain, who at one time was listed as having scored as many as 5.5 confirmed aerial victories, although newer lists have reduced this number to the single 3 December victory.

On Christmas Eve, future five-kill ace Lt Paul Bechtel of the 12th FS, claimed his first two victories. One of the Thirteenth Air Force's most unusual aces during the Solomons campaign, he had arrived on Guadalcanal to reinforce the island's air contingent late in November. During his subsequent tours of duty, Bechtel accounted for two Zeros in a P-39K-1, two more with a P-38G and a fifth confirmed victory in a US Marine Corps F4U-1 Corsair that he borrowed from VMF-124!

His first two kills were scored during a dive-bombing attack on Munda airstrip. Twenty-four Zeros had flown into the base during the night of 23 December, and the American fighter force of F4F Wildcats, P-39s and four P-38s of the newly-arrived 70th FS virtually wiped out the 14 Japanese fighters that managed to get airborne – US dive-bombers damaged or destroyed the remaining ten Zeros left on the ground.

Part of a flight of P-39s flying at 16,000 ft, Bechtel had spotted six Zeros climbing out of Munda as the fighter escorts approached the target area. Making effective use of his height advantage, he quickly closed on the tail of one of the enemy fighters but saw no hits from his first burst of fire. Having never previously fired his guns in anger, Bechtel reasoned that he was aiming behind the target, because the Japanese fighter continued on its way in a gentle turn. This allowed the future ace to fire an almost no-deflection shot, which in turn caused the Zero to burst into flames and eventually

A 12th FS P-39D basks in the shade of palm trees on Christmas Island in October 1942. The unit trained on this tropical paradise, situated between Hawaii and New Caledonia, prior to being sent to the hell that was Guadalcanal in November. Although the unit's total number of kills with the Airacobra tallied fewer than a dozen, its record supporting troops on the ground was exceptional. The 12th FS was commanded by future ace Maj Paul Bechtel throughout this period (*via Bell Textron*)

Pilots of the 70th FS prepare to board a Guadalcanal-bound C-47 in Fiji in December 1942. They are, standing from left to right, Joe Moore, George Toppol, Henry Viccello, A J Buck, Rex Barber, Dick Rivers and Bob Pettit. Squatting, from left to right, are Bill Daggit, Harvey Dunbar, Darrell Cosart, Tom Lanphier and Phil Hendrix (*Cosart via Cook*)

Paul Bechtel (third from right, sat on the wing) and his flight pose for a group shot alongside a 12th FS P-39. By the time the unit first deployed to Guadalcanal in December 1942, allied forces in the Solomons enjoyed a greater degree of aerial superiority than had been the case when the 67th FS arrived at Henderson Field in August. And although this meant that fewer aerial engagements took place, pilots actually stood more chance of success when Japanese aircraft were engaged (*via Ames*)

A 12th FS P-39D cruises over the Pacific during a training sortie from Christmas Island in mid-1942. The unit's gradual work-up to combat readiness was thrown into disarray following the US invasion of Guadalcanal in August 1942. Indeed, the truncated training programme which ensued meant that pilots were not properly prepared for action by the time they deployed into the frontline (*via Ames*)

crash into the sea. The aircraft's demise was witnessed by Bechtel's wingman.

Seemingly unaware of the P-39s' presence until this moment, the remaining Japanese pilots suddenly woke up to the damger and scattered like ducks off a pond. Bechtel's wingman warned him over the radio that a Zero was on his tail, and a single look over his shoulder confirmed this. The enemy's tracers were corkscrewing toward the P-39 when Bechtel pulled into a hard right turn – so hard that his fighter went into a spin. Having lost a considerable amount of height by the time he had arrested the spin, Bechtel now found himself all alone. Minutes later he spotted a solitary Zero, and after stalking it for a short time, he shot it down with a single burst. Bechtel's second kill was confirmed by US troops on the ground.

Having flown numerous fighter types in combat, Paul Bechtel was well qualified to comment on the effectiveness of the Airacobra;

'I had a lot of experience with the P-39, having first flown the YP-39 as early as 28 February 1941 at Patterson Field, Ohio. I flew it quite a bit thereafter, doing both accelerated service testing at Patterson Field and regular flying with my squadron, the 39th PS, which was the first unit in the army air corps to be equipped with P-39s. I logged more time on the P-39 after moving to Christmas Island in early 1942, where I trained new pilots posted to the 12th FS.

'Of all the aeroplanes that I flew, I rate the P-39 the best in so far as flying, ground handling, visibility and general performance are concerned. I was initially impressed, and satisfied, with its armament (guns and ammunition) until I got into combat. All the guns, except the 0.50-cals, were charged by pulling cables in the cockpit – two on the floor to the right of the seat for the 0.30s in the right wing, two on the floor to the left of the seat for the 0.30s in the left wing and two (a charger and a loader) on the centre console for the cannon. The synchronised 0.50s had handles on the right and left side of the instrument panel. In all cases, the hardest part of the charging pull was at the end of the pull, and that is where one physically had the least leverage.

'The 37 mm cannon never did work in a satisfactory manner in any of the outfits I flew with. It would jam after one to three shots, and usually the jam could not be cleared in the air. Every unit that could scrounge replacement 20 mm cannons would carry out a wholesale swap as quickly as possible. The Hispano 20 mm was standard in the P-400 (the British version of the P-39) and the P-38, and it was a reliable gun.'

Paul Bechtel eventually took command of the 12th FS after the Thirteenth Air Force was officially

More 12th FS P-39s 'on the wing' during squadron training in mid 1942. All of the unit's Airacobras appear to have been adorned both with female names and the official squadron badge (a hand clenching a lightning bolt). *Innocent Imogene* heads this formation – note the exposed belly tank shackles protruding from the underside of the fighter (*via Ames*)

This rare shot shows the regular mount of Bill Fiedler, who was the only American pilot to be credited with five aerial victories in the Airacobra. Photographed in early 1943, this P-39N has certainly seen better days. Considering the exploits of its pilot, the veteran fighter is remarkably free of personal or victory markings, aside from the skull and crossbones just to the right of the two-number aircraft code (*via Cook*)

activated on 13 January 1943, and the unit carried out whatever assignments their aircraft were best suited to. For the most part the P-39 pilots either escorted bombers striking targets in the northern Solomon Islands, or carried out low altitude interceptions and routine patrols.

And it was during this period that the sole American ace to score five aerial victories with a P-39 claimed all of his kills. The 70th FS's Lt William Fiedler shot down his first Zero whilst escorting B-17s sent to bomb Ballale Island on 26 January 1943. The following month the Japanese decided to evacuate the eastern end of the Solomon Islands, and Fiedler scored his second Zero kill on 4 February while escorting bombers sent to attack one of the retreating 'Tokyo Express' convoys.

Twenty-two Japanese destroyers and transports were detected sailing through 'the Slot', the narrow channel of water amidst the Solomon Islands chain. An American force of 28 fighters and 25 bombers was hastily scrambled to attack the Japanese ships, and whilst fighting their way through to the ships, a number of defending Zeros were shot down.

Capt James Robinson was leading a force of eight 70th FS P-39s on this mission, and he successfully bounced a Zero that exploded after being hit by an accurate burst of fire. A second navy fighter was credited to Robinson just minutes later, a Wildcat pilot watching the Zero fall in flames into the sea. William Fiedler followed his leader into the teeth of the Japanese escort, and managed to claim a Zero destroyed before the remaining fighters forced the Americans to break off their attack.

No further Airacobra kills were scored until June 1943, when the Japanese desperately tried to reverse the trend of Allied victories in the South Pacific. On the 12th of the month a massive sweep of 50 Zeros was met by more than 90 Allied fighters, and more than 30 Japanese aircraft were destroyed – Fiedler, who had transferred to the 68th FS in April, accounted for his third Zero during this action.

Four days later another large Japanese force was intercepted between Beaufort Bay and Cape Esperance, and again large numbers of enemy aircraft were destroyed, including two 'Val' dive-bombers claimed by Fiedler. His flight was the last to engage the enemy, and by then previous interceptions had effectively dispersed the dive-bombers' fighter escorts. This gave Fiedler's flight a relatively clear shot at the 'Vals', and six were claimed by the P-39 pilots.

Having quickly despatched one dive-bomber, Fiedler's scoring run was temporarily interrupted when the nose cannon and 0.50-in machine guns in his P-39K jammed. He was then forced to down his all-important fifth kill with only the four 0.30-in wing guns.

When debriefing after this one-sided mission, most American pilots agreed that their opponents on the day were obviously inexperienced because of the ineffective tactics employed by the Zero escorts. In the event, more than 30 Japanese aircraft were claimed by navy and marine pilots, while another 40+ were credited to Thirteenth Air Force squadrons. The total Japanese force engaged on this day was estimated to have totalled 90 fighters and bombers.

With his fifth kill under his belt, and a sudden upsurge in enemy air activity, Bill Fiedler looked set to become one of the great aces of the Thirteenth Air Force. However, exactly two weeks after attaining ace status, he was killed in a freak accident on Guadalcanal. Whilst sitting in his P-39 on a taxiway, waiting his turn to take off, Fiedler's P-39 was struck by a P-38 that had suffered engine failure just as it had become airborne. Both fighters exploded, and future P-40 ace Frank Gaunt of the 44th FS braved the flames to drag Fiedler's unconscious body from the blazing wreckage. The P-39 pilot was described as having been burned beyond recognition, and he died a few hours later.

Airacobra units based in the South Pacific will not be remembered for their contribution to the numerous fighter-vs-fighter combats that took place in 1942-43. And it is doubtful whether most pilots that swapped their P-39s and P-400s for other fighter types ever regretted leaving the Airacobra behind. However, the Bell fighter did fill a critical need for a low-level interceptor and ground attack platform during the desperate battles in the Solomons in late 1942 and early 1943.

Brig-Gen 'Chuck' Yeager's comment in the introduction about the quality of the fighter pilot taking precedence over the type of aeroplane he flies is understandable in light of Thirteenth Air Force experience in this theatre. There were a number of victories attributed to P-39s or P-400s in the struggle to recapture the Solomon Islands that reflected the fighting spirit of pilots such as John Mitchell or Bill Fiedler. That the Bell fighter did not score more victories in-theatre was due to its limited range, poor performance at altitude and the unreliability of its guns.

Still featuring a red circle within its fuselage star, this 70th FS P-39 was photographed on Fiji in early 1942 – the 'meatball' was officially removed in early May. Detachments from the squadron were sent to Guadalcanal from December 1942 onwards, with such legendary 70th FS aces as John Mitchell, Rex Barber and Tom Lanphier all seeing their first action in P-39s at this time. Mitchell claimed three aerial victories during his tour, whilst Barber and Lanphier each got one apiece. Most, if not all, of the P-39 pilots who participated in the Yamamoto interception mission of 18 April 1943 flew P-39s from Guadalcanal with the 70th FS during this period (*via Douglas Canning*)

FINAL VICTORIES IN THE SOUTHWEST PACIFIC

By the end of 1943 all Airacobra units in New Guinea had transitioned to other types, Thirteenth Fighter Command having replaced most of its P-39s with P-38s by the last quarter of the year, and V Fighter Command losing its Bell fighters just prior to Christmas. The P-39 would remain in production for the Soviets, however.

Returning to the start of 1943, the 80th FS had claimed its seventh, and final, P-39 kill in New Guinea on 17 January. This had taken the form of a Ki-21 'Sally' bomber downed near Fergusson Island, on the eastern tip of New Guinea, by future 22-kill P-38 ace Jay T Robbins and Gerald Rogers. Both pilots put numerous bursts of gunfire into the aircraft, and duly watched it crash. However, with no fractional credits being granted by the Fifth Air Force, the two men decided the issue on the flip of a coin, and Rogers won! Robbins was officially credited with having damaged two Ki-21s on this date.

Perhaps the most impressive missions flown by V Fighter Command P-39s occurred between February and August 1943. Conditions were favourable to the Americans on at least three occasions during this time, and P-39 pilots took full advantage by claiming more than 40

Lt Bill McDonough's P-39K-1 42-4358 is seen on the flightline at Nadzab in early 1943. The future five-kill ace used this very aircraft to down two Zeros (with a third probably destroyed) during the epic battle over Wau on 6 February 1943. As the lower photograph on this page shows, 42-4358 wore a large nose-art of 'Donald Duck' on its right side, which was clearly not duplicated on the left. For some reason, many V Fighter Command pilots preferred to decorate the right side of their aircraft rather than the traditional left (*via* Krane)

The size of the nose-art of McDonough's Airacobra is readily apparent in this view, which shows the future ace (far right) with his groundcrewmen, Sgts Palzuski and Pierce. McDonough would achieve ace status with a further three kills whilst flying P-47Ds with the 35th FG in February-March 1944. Completing his combat tour the following month, and having been promoted to the rank of major, McDonough was killed when his parachute failed after he bailed out of a Thunderbolt near Port Moresby on 22 April. He was just days away from boarding a transport back to the US when the accident happened (*via* Krane)

of the 50 kills credited to USAAF units between these months.

Much of this action took place overhead the advanced airstrip at Wau, which was only a few miles south of the enemy stronghold at Lae. Realising the importance of this base, the Japanese mounted a series of raids to 'remove this thorn in their side'. Savage fighting took place all around Wau at the end of January, with the Japanese finally conceding the use of the base to their enemies after they had suffered heavy losses.

Despite having lost the battle for Wau on the ground, the enemy continued to bomb and strafe the airstrip well into the middle of 1943. Aside from opposing these

raids, the P-39 pilots of the 40th and 41st FSs would additionally enjoy notable successes whilst protecting C-47 transports shuttling supplies and reinforcements into the base.

One such action took place on 6 February, when both units intercepted a large formation of seven Ki-21s, escorted by 21 Japanese Army Air Force Ki-43 'Oscars'. Eight P-39s of the 40th FS were escorting C-47s over the Wau area at the time, and they found themselves in a sound tactical position from which to 'bounce' the Ki-43s. Attacking from above, the American pilots fell on the enemy with all guns blazing, and 11 Japanese fighters and one Ki-21 fell to the P-39s' withering fire. Lt Edwin Schneider was eventually given credit for the destruction of two fighters and the 'Sally' to gain top honours for the engagement, whilst future ace Bill McDonough opened his account with two Ki-43s. The only USAAF losses were one C-47 shot down and a second forced to crash-land. The battle had lasted from 1045 hrs until the P-39s withdrew at 1100 hrs.

Just after midday, a flight of P-39s from the 41st FS started patrolling over Wau, and it too ran into more Ki-43s. Four were claimed for no loss, with future ace Lt Frank Dubisher claiming the first of his five victories during this fight (he was credited with downing a 'Zero'). Commander of the Fifth Air Force, Gen George Kenney, was so elated with the day's results that he deliberately downplayed press releases to avoid sceptics on the home front criticising his units for overclaiming.

Other large air raids were directed at the Port Moresby and Oro Bay areas in succeeding months, with one of the largest Japanese efforts

Another pilot to claim two kills during the 6 February 1943 clash over Wau was the 40th FS's Lt Thomas Winburn, who downed a pair of Ki-43s (*via Krane*)

Lt Gene DeBoer also claimed an 'Oscar' during the fight on 6 February. As with Winburn's fighter, this machine has been parked beneath its own personal canvas covering, which kept the cockpit cool and gave the hard-working groundcrew a modicum of protection from the elements whilst carrying out maintenance on the P-39's mid-mounted engine. Note that the aircraft has had its 37 mm cannon replaced with a Hispano 20 mm weapon (*via Krane*)

Not all things went as planned in the frontline. Here, a 40th FS P-39 has come to grief whilst landing at Nadzab, the fighter almost certainly having suffered a nose gear failure. The rough airstrips in-theatre played havoc with the Airacobra's tricycle undercarriage; the fighter not enjoying the reputation for ruggedness synonymous with other American types such as the P-40 and P-47 (*via Krane*)

Two P-39Q-5s of the 36th FS patrol over Port Moresby in late 1943. Both aircraft have 0.50-cal machine guns in pods under the wings, plus a solitary 75-US gal centreline drop tank apiece. Note also the 'star and bar' marking, which was introduced in the autumn of 1943

This orderly line-up of 35th FG P-39N-2s was photographed at one of the airfields dotted around Port Moresby in early 1943. Conditions at these sites remained decidedly crude until the end of 1942, when the opening of new bases at Dobodura saw buildings such as nipa huts and control towers erected for the first time. Those fighters with dark-coloured (red) fin tips and propeller hubs belonged to the 40th FS, whilst those in yellow were assigned to the 41st FS (*via Krane*)

taking place on 12 April. A large formation of bombers, escorted by numerous fighters, was detected heading for Port Moresby, but fortunately the defending fighters of the V Fighter Command received warning of this attack early enough to effect a successful interception. At least 25 aircraft were downed, with the Airacobras of the 35th FG being credited with almost half the total claims – conversely, the only USAAF losses suffered were a pair of P-39s.

With the initiative now heavily in the Allies' favour, US fighters were now frequently seeking combat over enemy territory. Consequently, shorter-range fighters such as the P-39 and P-40s were often left to perform less glamorous missions such as local patrols or transport escort. The 35 P-39s of the 35th FG still saw plenty of action, however, as their new base at Wau continued to be subjected to Japanese attack. The group had taken up residence during the evening of 14 August 1943, and the very next morning, at 0910 hrs, a large force of Ki-48 'Lily' bombers, escorted by 'Oscars', approached Wau just as C-47s, escorted by P-39s, were

Above and top
Crews from the 35th and 36th FSs pose during a lull in the fighting at Milne Bay in late 1942. With the fighting having generally moved further northwest towards Buna by year-end, the hard-pressed crews from both units were able to luxuriate in pastimes such as having their pictures taken (*via Steve Maksymyk and Jim Walker*)

landing. Two of the transports were lost, along with their cargoes of men and material, but the P-39s of the 41st FS quickly exacted revenge by claiming at least ten 'Lilys' and up to three 'Oscars' destroyed.

Frank Dubisher was credited with the most spectacular score of the day, claiming three Ki-48s destroyed in the Tsili-Tsili area, whilst Lt Bob Alder destroyed two 'Lilys' and Lt Carey Wooley got yet another Ki-48 and an 'Oscar'.

About five minutes after the fight had begun, a flight of 40th FS fighters also found themselves embroiled in a scrap in the same general area, and within minutes three 'Lilys' and an 'Oscar' had been shot down – the Ki-43 and one of the Ki-48s were credited to future ace Lt Bob Yaeger, flying P-39N-5 42-19012. Although these victories had resulted in the P-39 enjoying one of its most productive days with V Fighter Command, the 35th FG had lost four Airacobras and three pilots.

An informal shot of two 80th FS groundcrewmen with their P-400 taken during the squadron's Milne Bay deployment, which lasted from late 1942 through to the end of January 1943. Badly hit by malaria, the 80th was the obvious candidate to become the first unit within the 8th FG to convert to P-38s. Indeed, its ranks were so depleted that its effectiveness as a frontline unit had been seriously comprised by early 1943 (*via 80th FS Association*)

The 41st FS's Lt W A Hymovich is seen flying his P-39N-5 (42-18815), nicknamed *Whiskey Pete*, in early 1943. Hymovich scored one of the last Airacobra victories for his unit when he claimed an 'Oscar' shot down on 26 November 1943 (*via Krane*)

This fuzzy still (of P-39D-2 41-38486) was taken from a cine film showing Airacobras from the 36th FS scrambling from a base near Port Moresby in August 1943. By this stage in the war the P-39 had been largely relegated to secondary duties such as transport escort, convoy cover or short-range ground attack. The 36th would retain P-39s until November 1943 (*via Krane*)

With Allied forces pushing the Japanese further north with every passing month, P-39 units were struggling to take the fight to the enemy due to the Bell fighter's modest range. The same problem was reducing the effectiveness of the P-40 and, to a lesser degree, the P-47. Indeed, by the final year of the war only the 'long-legged' P-38 and P-51D/K had sufficient range to cover the distances being flown in the Pacific by V Fighter Command – hence almost all of its units flew either Lightnings or Mustangs by late 1944.

Future Medal of Honor winner Capt Bill Shomo poses with his veteran P-39Q-6 42-20351 at Biak, in New Guinea, in late 1944. Fitted with K-24 and K-25 aerial cameras in the aft fuselage, the photo-recce Airacobras performed sterling work in the Pacific theatre with the 71st Tactical Reconnaissance Group (TRG) until replaced by F-6D Mustangs in November 1944. A high-time P-39 pilot with the 71st TRG's 82nd TRS, Shomo won his Medal of Honor in an F-6D (nicknamed *Snooks 5th*) when he shot down seven Japanese aircraft during a single mission on 11 January 1945 (*via Krane*)

Yet despite its lack of range, and reduced mission effectiveness, the P-39 continued to be flown enthusiastically on operations in the Pacific through to the end of 1943.

Although the fighter's service with the Fifth and Thirteenth Air Forces was coming to an end, the Bell fighter still managed to score a few kills prior to leaving the frontline. With the demise of the fighter variants, the only Aircobras left in-theatre come 1944 were a handful of photo-recce-modified P-39Q-6s that were replaced by F-6D Mustangs in November of that year.

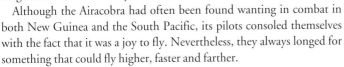

Frank Dubisher was a highly popular figure within the 41st FS, serving with the unit from September 1942 through to March 1944, by which time he had become CO. Having scored his first kill (a Ki-43, although it is officially recorded as a Zero) in P-400 BW111 during the Wau engagement of 6 February 1943, 'Duby' claimed a further three 'Lily' bombers on 15 August in P-39N-5 42-18802. He 'made ace' in a P-47D-11 on 13 March 1944, and left the 41st to become Executive Officer of the entire 35th FG later that same day. Dubisher, who would retire from the post-war USAF with the rank of lieutenant-colonel, passed away in Oregon in March 2000 (*via Cook*)

Although the Airacobra had often been found wanting in combat in both New Guinea and the South Pacific, its pilots consoled themselves with the fact that it was a joy to fly. Nevertheless, they always longed for something that could fly higher, faster and farther.

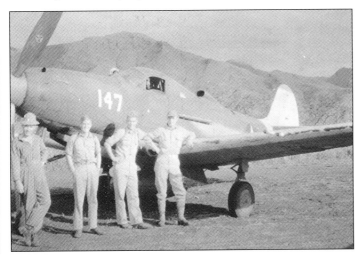

Bob Yaeger, Bill Gray, Richard Schmalz and Lt Pierce pose in front of the former's P-39 at Tsili-Tsili in early August 1943. Yaeger, who claimed a Ki-48 and Ki-43 near Wau on 15 August in P-39N-5 42-19012 (possibly 'White 147'?), would go on to score three more kills in a 40th FS P-47 on 11 March 1944 (*via Krane*)

ALEUTIANS, ICELAND, CANAL ZONE AND THE MTO

Several theatres during World War 2 saw little contact with the enemy, and life was hell for an aggressive young fighter pilot sent to these areas on active duty. The poor weather of the Aleutians or the boredom of mundane patrols over the Panama Canal, posed a far greater, and real, threat than enemy fighters. And with more than enough fighting for all seemingly taking place in the Southwest Pacific and, later, North Africa, all those eager young pilots could do was wait for the opportunity to transfer into a unit that experienced regular combat.

Yet another of those places that saw very little action was Iceland, which welcomed several squadrons of American warplanes following the US occupation of the island in mid-1942. This move followed in the wake of an agreement that had been reached with Great Britain, wherein American troops and equipment would use the bases on

P-39N-0 42-8926 was deployed to the Alaskan area in early 1943. Bell commenced production of the N-model in late 1942, and this particular aircraft was one of the first P-39Ns to be accepted by the USAAF (*via Bell Textron*)

This P-39J (41-7073) was the mount of 57th FS/54th FG pilot Lt Leslie Spoonts during the second half of 1942. Flying from Kodiak Island, Alaska, during the Aleutians campaign, Spoonts claimed to have downed three Japanese aircraft during his tour – note the victory symbols below the cockpit. There are no official records to back up his claims, however
(*via Michael O'Leary*)

This Airacobra was photographed soon after it had landed in Iceland in early 1942 – note the red centre to its national marking. A handful of P-39s saw sporadic action from Iceland during 1942 and 1943 when several marauding German reconnaissance aircraft approached closely enough to the island for them to be intercepted by short-range American fighters. These engagements resulted in several claims being made by P-39 pilots (*via Bell Textron*)

the island, thus releasing British troops for combat duty. In July and August a number of P-38s, P-39s and P-40s arrived to become part of the 342nd Composite Group (CG), formed on 11 September 1942.

Several future aces who later served in more active combat zones had their initiation to operational missions during the routine patrols over the convoys that came into range of Iceland. One such pilot was John C Meyer of the 33rd FS, who later distinguished himself as a top Mustang ace with the Eighth Air Force, claiming some 24 aerial kills.

Meyer's Icelandic unit had been one of the first to arrive on the island during August 1942, and had participated in the USAAF's very first aerial kill in the European Theater of Operations (ETO) on the 15th of that month. A P-38 of the 27th FS was staging through Iceland on its way to England when it caught a four-engine Fw 200 patrolling over the North Atlantic. The official record reads something like 'a pilot from the 33rd FS attacked the Fw 200, setting it aflame, before the Lightning made a fast gunnery pass that exploded the German bomber'.

It is not entirely clear whether the 'pilot from the 33rd FS', Lt Joseph Shaffer, was flying a P-39 or a P-40 on this mission, for the unit had brought P-39s to Iceland, but also apparently used Warhawks during 1942. Indeed, some sources specify a P-40 as the victorious type on this mission, but it is more likely that Shaffer was using one of the Airacobras flown to Iceland just a few days earlier.

Aircraft type aside, some members of the 33rd still heatedly insist that Lt Shaffer had 'bagged' the German aeroplane before the P-38 pilot ever got into range. Although the facts concerning who shot the Fw 200 down in which type of aircraft remain unclear, there is no question that the P-39D-equipped 33rd FS had participated in the first USAAF victory in the ETO. Ironically, Joseph Shaffer also scored the unit's only other victory when he claimed a Ju 88 on 18 October 1942 . . . in a P-39D.

At the same time that the 342nd CG was seeing action against the Germans for the first time, the 28th CG, comprising elements of the 54th and 343rd FGs, was engaging Japanese forces that had invaded the Aleutians. And just as the fighter pilots of the 342nd had encountered little

43

opposition over the cold North Atlantic, their brethren in Alaska found few Japanese aircraft over the cold waters of the Aleutians – total claims by war's end amounted to just 30 Japanese aircraft shot down.

The bulk of these victories fell to the P-39, the type undertaking the base defence role in the Alaskan theatre. Further Airacobra units were flown in on a temporary basis following the Japanese diversionary invasion of the Aleutians, and once the Allies had recaptured the islands of Kiska and Attu in mid-1943, most P-39 squadrons returned to their continental US bases.

Although the most successful Airacobra pilots in the area never scored more than two confirmed victories, many of them went on to become successful P-38 aces with the 49th FG in the Southwest Pacific. Men such as Tom McGuire (38 kills), Wallace Jordan (6 kills) and Jerry Johnson (22 kills) all saw their first action in P-39s of the 54th FG in the Aleutians in 1942-43, with McGuire actually enduring a forced landing in the bitter cold of Alaska during his five-month tour.

Jerry Johnson was the most successful of the three in the Aleutians, claiming a 'Rufe' destroyed (and a second as a probable) in the Adak-Kiska area on 25 September and a second fighter in the same area six days later. Oddly enough, Johnson's parent Eleventh Air Force granted only probable destroyed status for the claims, but Fifth Air Force tallies list them as confirmed – there is no documentation for either claim within the records of Johnson's 57th FS.

The first of these 'kills' had been achieved when the 57th strafed two Japanese submarines, a number of biplanes on the water and a large transport vessel near the islands of Kiska and Attu. Two of the 'Rufe' floatplane fighters that had tried to prevent these attacks were claimed shot down, while another was credited to Johnson as probably destroyed. He had now opened his scoring tally, which would eventually total 20 victories with the P-38, two with the P-47 and perhaps two more with the P-39.

Fighter pilots were generally assigned Aleutians duty for a little over one year before they were allowed to transfer to more active theatres. And the seemingly endless patrols flown over freezing ocean in some of the world's dirtiest weather prepared these pilots for later aerial combat in either the Pacific or the ETO/MTO.

Although boasting far better weather, the Panama Canal Zone saw even less fighter action than the Aleutians. The Sixth Air Force maintained a defence against submarine and air attacks on the locks from early 1942 onwards, and despite German submarines being detected on several occasions, no aerial engagements ever took place. Again, the burden of aerial defence for the canal zone fell to P-39s, P-40s and later P-38s.

Both Medal of Honor winner Neel Kearby and future P-47 ace Bill 'Dinghy' Dunham served in the Canal Zone, as well as Bob Goehausen, who later became a Mustang ace in the Mediterranean Theater of

Jerry Johnson's P-39D-1 41-38295 is seen in flight over the Aleutians in late 1942. It was whilst serving in this theatre that Johnson earned the nickname 'Johnny Eager' due to his zealous desire for aerial combat. Despite only engaging enemy aircraft on a handful of occasions in the Aleutians, Johnson nonetheless sharpened his combat skills at the controls of his P-39, and he went on to become one of the most formidable fighter pilots in the Pacific (*via John Bruning*)

With little fear of being attacked by surprise from the air, the groundcrewmen refuelling this 32nd FS P-39N-5 at a base in the Panama Canal Zone go about their work in the open at a pre-war pace. Such a sight could never have been repeated in the Southwest Pacific or the MTO, where groundcrews were constantly wary of sudden enemy air raids. Indeed, aircraft in areas within reach of enemy warplanes needed elaborate dispersal to ensure minimum damage during attacks from the air (*W K Giroux*)

The 32nd FS's William 'Kenny' Giroux models his regulation flying gear prior to flying yet another boring canal patrol. His mount is a camouflaged P-39N-5, which has been adorned with a unit badge on the cockpit door (over which is slung the pilot's parachute pack and life jacket). Giroux would transfer to the Southwest Pacific in late 1943 after continually pestering his commanding officer for a posting to a true combat zone (*W K Giroux*)

Operations (MTO). Some of the fighter units were based on Aruba or Puerto Rico, while other detachments were stationed in Panama itself.

Another pilot destined to become an ace (this time on P-38s with V Fighter Command over the Philippines in 1944) was William K Giroux, who spent six months in Panama flying P-39s with the 30th and 32nd FSs. Joining the 8th FG's 36th FS in New Guinea in August 1943, he initially flew P-39s once again, before transitioning firstly onto the P-47 and then the P-38 – he claimed ten kills with the latter type between March and November 1944. A highly experienced fighter pilot, Giroux expressed his views on the P-39 in Bill Hess's *Pacific Sweep*;

'It took no time to realise that I had a poor combat aeroplane. It had served its purpose well in Panama, but this was a brand-new ball game. The P-39 had no range to get you where the real action was, poor service ceiling, poor rate of climb, and it wasn't the best in a dive. Consequently, we drew the poorest missions – strafing and short-range escort for the transports.'

The MTO was another theatre where the P-39 served well – albeit mostly in less than glorious missions

such as convoy patrol or armed reconnaissance. There were very few victories scored by Airacobra pilots in-theatre, with different victory lists awarding between 14 and 20 kills for 107 P-39s lost to all causes. By comparison, USAAF P-40 pilots in-theatre were credited with just over 480 aerial victories for 553 losses.

Amongst the select few P-39 pilots in the MTO to go on and 'make ace' was Lt Ben Emmert, who served with the 154th TRS prior to joining the 325th FG's 318th FS in January 1944, and going on to score six kills in Thunderbolts and Mustangs.

Although Emmert failed to claim any victories with the Airacobra in the MTO, fellow pilot Hugh Dow achieved this unique feat whilst flying P-39Ls with the 350th FG's 346th FS, which had deployed to North Africa from England in January 1943. Operating over the Kasserine Pass, the young Lt Dow did not have long to wait for his first aerial combat. On the morning of 15 February he had literally just taken off on a ground attack mission from Thelepte field, flying as wingman to his flight leader, when he spotted fiery explosions erupting below him. Dow then spied several Bf 109s climbing away from their strafing run, and he duly followed his leader as he chased after the unsuspecting enemy fighters.

The two P-39 pilots quickly caught them up and attacked a pair of German fighters, damaging them both. Breaking off his attack, Dow looked around and saw a third Bf 109 speeding away from the airfield, and with some effort he managed to close to within firing range. He remembers;

Lt Hugh Dow poses alongside the cockpit of his 346th FS P-39L-1 in the spring of 1943 (*via Dow*)

'Naturally, my 37 mm cannon had jammed on the pass I had made at the first '109. We had a T-handle in the middle of the cockpit floor, and by pulling a cable out to just past your right ear you could get another round into the chamber. I had the presence of mind to execute that manoeuvre as I closed up behind him. I had decided that I would wait until I was right on top of him before giving him a blast.

'He had drifted up to 200-300 ft by now, and must have finally seen me, because he suddenly hit the deck again. I dropped down immediately, and as I bounced around in his slipstream I finally squeezed off a burst. There were strikes all over his aircraft and I immediately overran him as his power came off. A few seconds later as I chopped power and rolled up to look at him, he hit the ground in a ball of smoke and dust.'

Dow was pleased to learn that the German pilot, Unteroffizier Karl Reinbacher of III./JG 77, had survived the crash and was in the custody of French troops. The Americans convinced their allies that the prisoner was needed for interrogation, and he was handed over. When Reinbacher was introduced to his victor the German presented an admiring salute.

By April 1944 the 350th FG was one of the last P-39-equipped groups in the whole USAAF, and on the 6th of that month Hugh Dow scored what was almost certainly the Airacobra's final aerial victory. Leading a flight sent to bomb rail and road bridges across a river south of Grossetto, in Italy, he had just pulled away from the target after dropping his ordnance when he spotted a Bf 109 ahead of him to his left. The two adversaries quickly turned into each other for a head-on attack.

Since scoring his first kill in February 1943, Dow had been able to test fly a captured Messerschmitt fighter, and he knew that his chances of out-turning the enemy aircraft were good at low altitude. He was betting with his life, but Dow was right, as his P-39 gained about 90 degrees of deflection on the Bf 109 in just a single turn. With long streamers of condensation rolling off the wings of the German fighter as its pilot tried to stay with the P-39, Dow calmly eased in behind his foe for a minimum deflection shot at close range. However, having been strafing targets earlier in the mission, Dow was out of cannon ammunition and short of every other kind.

He fired his guns until all the 0.50-cal rounds were gone, and then he peppered his hapless victim with the four 'thirties' in the wings. The Bf 109 finally burst into flames and shot up in a zoom stall, with Dow glued to his tail, continuing to fire. The fighter was now ablaze, and the German pilot braved the continuing hail of bullets and bailed out at low altitude – his Bf 109 practically crashed into the bridge that the P-39s had just bombed.

Hugh Dow claimed two Bf 109s during his long tour in the MTO, the first of which was flown by Unteroffizier Karl Reinbacher (second from left) of III./JG 77

47

Despite seeing action in the MTO from late 1942 through to mid-1944, few photos of Airacobras in-theatre have surfaced over the years. This P-39N-0 has the short-lived yellow-ringed national marking synonymous with the MTO (*Howard Levy via Jerry Scutts*)

Two anonymous P-39N-2s beat up their airfield at the end of a sortie in early 1943 (*Howard Levy via Jerry Scutts*)

With two kills to his credit, Hugh Dow was one of the highest scoring P-39 pilots in the MTO, and he would go on to command the 347th FS after it converted to P-47s – his long tour eventually came to an end in January 1945 when he was shot down and made a PoW. The mission of 6 April 1944 was probably the last time USAAF P-39s scored aerial victories, and the 350th gave the fighter a fitting send off by downing five German fighters for no losses.

As previously noted, some 107 P-39s were lost in the MTO to all causes, with most of these being downed by groundfire. In return, sources quote up to 20 confirmed claims in the air and about the same number on the ground. And although USAAF P-40s claimed about 500 enemy air-craft in the air and on the ground for about 550 losses, the P-39 flew about half as many missions as the Warhawk, and enjoyed a loss rate of about 0.4 per sortie. The heavily-favoured P-40 had a loss rate of 0.8 per sortie, but remained a much more tractable opponent in the hands of motivated American fighter pilots.

By the end of the war, the P-39 had offered valuable service, even though it was not to be one of the star performers in the Pacific or Mediterranean theatres. At best it was a good substitute for the subsequent generation of American fighters that appeared later in the war, and although derided by many that flew it, the Bell fighter was capable of doing the job for which it was designed when flown by well-motivated and skilled pilots. The remaining chapters in this volume prove just that.

93rd FS/81st FG pilot Lt Alexander Yankaskas poses on the wing of his P-39 in the autumn of 1943. This photograph was taken after the North African campaign had ended, and the score on his fighter should technically have comprised just one swastika, for USAF records indicate that his sole official kill was an Me 210 claimed on 24 June 1943 (*via Carl Molesworth*)

SOVIET KOBRAS

Although the P-39 was unloved in the Pacific, except by Japanese fighter pilots, who generally enjoyed a meeting with the type, elsewhere it proved far more dangerous. Indeed, Soviet pilots even succeeded in taking on the formidable Focke-Wulf Fw 190, as legendary German ace Walter Nowotny recounts;

'This area, dotted with several Soviet landing strips, has always been a good hunting ground in the past. We don't have to wait long today either. Ahead to the left, a few tiny specks emerge from the mist in the far distance. They quickly get bigger and reveal themselves as a gaggle of 20 Soviet ground-attack aircraft. A few moments later we spot six more machines, American (P-39) fighters, flying escort.

'We are flying at about 1000 m, with the Soviets some 200 m below us – their escort is about 1200 m. I immediately climb to get above them. The sun is in the south-west. The "Americans", now below me, haven't noticed anything. I get one in my sights and open fire – he immediately dives away on fire, hitting the ground in a burst of flame. Startled, the remaining five curve away to the right. I have achieved my object. The fighters are now some 500 to 600 metres away from the ground-attackers, and my men have a clear field.

'Meanwhile, as I try for another fighter, they are attempting to get on my tail. They end up in a circle, with me in the middle trying to get into position for a good shot. We are all gradually losing height. I hardly fire a shot, while behind me one or two of the opposition loose off wildly at me – at much too great a range and far wide of the mark. Then, at about 50 m off the ground, I get the second one in my sights. He too immediately goes into the ground in a ball of flame.

'I look over my shoulder. The fight has taken a nasty turn. Eight Soviet fighters have arrived on the scene and join in the proceedings! I am sitting on the tail of one of the "Americans". Behind me is one of the Soviets. A few quick glances convince me he is getting closer.

'To my right a line of bullet holes suddenly appears in my wing. The Soviet is letting fly with everything he has got. His firing hardly stops. A cannon shell smashes into my wing, tearing open the surface. Ivan is getting closer and closer. He's almost within ramming distance.

This aircraft was amongst the first batch of Airacobra Is sent to the Soviet Union in January 1942, being assigned to 19 GIAP. Still wearing its British serial AN619, it was flown by Jr Lt V V Gabrinets until lost in action during 1942 (*via Petrov*)

Whenever I glance behind me, the huge Soviet star seems to fill my vision. Bullets continue to hit my wing. They are getting closer to my cockpit.

'The moment of decision has come. I take one last chance and dump as much speed as I dare. I use all the skill and expertise I have gained in my many previous dogfights to hold her steady as my speed sinks suddenly and dangerously low.

'Fifty metres ahead of me is the "American", little more than ten metres behind me the Russian. Throughout the chase I have been slipping to the right in an attempt to dodge my pursuer's shots. I try the same manoeuvre one last time. And this time Ivan falls for it. For a split-second, as I wallow once more to the right at little more than a stall, he loses concentration. I take two more cannon hits before I complete the manoeuvre, but then he has overshot me, flashing past beneath my wings.

'He appears ahead of me. I clearly see the pilot in his cockpit, the Soviet star. I ram home the throttle – full power! I hope the good old Focke-Wulf, hurt though she is, can take it! Within a trice I am on top of the Russian. He goes down under my first burst of fire. The duel is over. The whole fight has lasted exactly 45 minutes. After a successful landing, I climb out of my machine drenched in sweat. I examine the damage in silence. It was worse than I had realised. Half the rudder is missing and one aileron shot to pieces. My main undercarriage tyres are bullet-holed and one cylinder and cylinder head completely shot away. More damage to the engine, bullet-riddled wings . . .'

Although this battle had ended with several victories for Nowotny, it is obvious that these kills were due solely to his skill as a pilot, and not to any deficiencies in the opposing aircraft. In many other battles, even against the top German *experten*, the outcome favoured the Russians in their P-39s.

INTO ACTION

Two weeks after the Airacobra entered combat over the South Pacific, it began a glorious career on the Soviet front. It is interesting to observe that the *Kobra*, as the Russians called it, first saw service on secondary fronts in the far north and south, and only later operated over the main fronts in the centre. Although the P-39 failed as a fighter everywhere else, in Russia it was so successful that toward the end of the war some of the leading Soviet aces even resisted transition to later, more modern native aircraft.

In the wake of the destruction of the Soviet Air Forces in the first weeks of the war, British Prime Minister Winston Churchill quickly offered to send fighters to the Communists in order to help them stave off defeat. The RAF did not have enough Spitfires for itself in mid-1941, and duly could spare none for Russia, so the first assistance sent consisted of sec-ondhand Hurricanes, which began arriving at Murmansk in late July.

Very quickly the RAF decided that it could also spare some of its lend-lease Tomahawks and Kittyhawks, as well as all of the Airacobra Is which had not already been returned to the United States. The first Bell fighters were shipped to Murmansk at the end of December 1941, with more following in 1942. The British sent 212 Airacobra Is in all via the northern route to Murmansk, 54 of which were lost en route.

The first 20 Airacobra Is were assigned to 22 ZAP (*Zapasnii Aviatsionii Polk* – Reserve or Depot Aviation Regiment), which had been established in October 1941 at Ivanovo, north-east of Moscow, to provide training on lend-lease fighters, and one more was given to the NII-VVS (*Nauchno-issledovatelnii Institut VVS* – The Air Force Scientific Research Institute) for experimental evaluation.

At this time the usual Soviet practice was to leave a regiment at the front until all its aircraft had been lost, and then withdraw the surviving pilots to a ZAP in the rear, where they would receive new aircraft and replacement pilots, before returning to the front for another cycle of operations. 22 ZAP was established with three squadrons, one each providing training on the Hurricane, Airacobra and Kittyhawk. Later, it would be grouped with similarly-tasked 14 ZAP within 6 ZAB (*Brigada*).

In November 1942 Transcaucasus-based 25 ZAP was assigned to introduce lend-lease types coming in through the Persian Gulf corridor, and it was equipped with P-39D/K versions of the Bell fighter. Exactly one year later 26 ZAP was created with the P-39M/N/Q.

In contrast to ZAPs for domestic aircraft types, 22 ZAP also had to assemble the lend-lease aircraft prior to flying them. This initially proved to be a difficult task because the Airacobras came with only limited documentation, all of which was in English, and much of the construction and early flying proceeded on the basis of trial and error.

One peculiarity of a number of the early P-39 units, both those flying in the north with the Airacobra I and in the Caucasus with the P-39D/K, was that they were not pure *Kobra* regiments. Indeed, during 1942 some units receiving the Bell fighter were also required to take on a squadron of P-40s, which resulted in regiments operating two squadrons of P-39s alongside one of Kittyhawks! This mix created no particular tactical advantage for the unit, nor did the VVS actually desire the additional logistical and maintenance problems. However, the P-39 was the more desired aircraft, and there were not enough of them to go around.

From 1943, when both *Kobras* and Kittyhawks became available in quantity, regiments began to equip exclusively with one or the other type, with the P-39s going to the most prestigious and highest priority units. Training and re-equipment of IAPs (*Istrebitelnyi Aviatsionnii Polk* – Fighter Aviation Regiment) began in April 1942, and 153 and 185 IAPs returned to the front with Airacobras at the end of June 1942. By then, however, 19 GIAP had entered combat with the Bell fighter.

Initially formed as 145 IAP in Karelia in January 1940, the unit had seen action during the Winter War with Finland, losing five aircraft and claiming five kills – Soviet units seriously overclaimed during this conflict, and the 145 IAP's actual victories were probably somewhere between none and two. When the Germans invaded in June 1941, the regiment was equipped with I-16s at Vaenga, in the far north, and its location spared it from the worst of the initial surprise attacks.

During the subsequent months 145 IAP distinguished itself flying the I-16, MiG-3, LaGG-3 and Hurricane, and on 7 March 1942 it was honoured with Guards status as 19 GIAP. In April the redesignated unit was briefly withdrawn from the front to Afrikanda Airbase to receive new aircraft. Instead of going to a ZAP, however, the regiment was issued with crated aircraft taken directly from railcars, which the unit's engineering staff, working in the open under primitive arctic conditions, firstly had to assemble. The first test flight of an Airacobra I was made on 19 April by Capt Pavel Kutakhov, commander of the regiment's first squadron.

An unidentified Soviet pilot enters his P-39. Although the Bell fighter's 'car door' was considered dangerous when it came to bailing out, the Airacobra's clear-view cockpit glazing was warmly welcomed by the Russians. By comparison, home-built fighters were fitted with poor quality, cellulose-based, transparencies throughout the war. These tended to quickly yellow with exposure to the sun and elements, and thus become less that completely transparent. This problem, and the occasional malfunction of the canopy sliding mechanism on most Soviet-built designs, encouraged many pilots to fly with their hoods back, or even entirely removed, in spite of the deleterious effect this had on aircraft performance and on pilot comfort (*via Russian Aviation Research Trust*)

Although the Russian pilots were initially bothered by the fighter's unfamiliar tricycle landing gear, they were soon won over when they discovered that it gave them much better control of the aircraft on the ground and drastically improved their forward vision when taxying. The *Kobra* was also far superior to any other fighter when it came to taxying across snowy landing fields. Once airborne, the aircraft's top speed and rate of climb were superior to the regiment's previous equipment, and the all-around vision canopy also proved useful in the air – even more so on account of the high quality of the Western cockpit transparency.

The Russians also found the *Kobra's* cockpit roomy, warm and comfortable in comparison to the fighters they had flown before – not a small matter for sub-arctic flying. Another feature much appreciated by the communist pilots was the aircraft's superior radio, an example of which was placed in every fighter. At the time, most older Russian fighters had no radio at all, whilst the newer ones had inadequate sets. In fact those fitted to most MiGs, LaGGs and Yaks could only receive, whilst radios capable of both receiving and transmitting were only made available to formation leaders, and both types of radio rarely worked at all.

This deficiency is at least a partial explanation for some of the outdated tactics long used by the VVS. With a general availability of two-way radios for all P-39s, more complex and open formations became possible. The employment of this equipment also meant that junior pilots who spotted enemy aircraft could give a warning to their comrades, thus allowing unit leaders to modify their formations – and tactics – in flight. It may not be completely by chance that some of the most innovative tactics developed by Russian pilots were assigned to Airacobra units.

The Soviet pilots' feeling about the armament was more ambivalent. They liked the 20 mm cannon, but found the British 7.7 mm (0.303-in) machine guns too light a calibre – 'good only for damaging German paint' they complained. Frequently, pilots had the latter removed entirely, stating that the weight saved was better than any firepower lost.

When the Russians received later model P-39s with 37 mm cannon, they liked the type even more, and they even considered the 0.50-cal machine guns acceptable. In fact, by Soviet standards, two heavy machine guns and a single cannon was an armament equal or superior to that of most of their domestic fighters. And when the P-39Q arrived with 0.50-cal guns in underwing gondolas, these were removed by the Russians.

The P-39's manoeuvrability, particularly in the vertical plane, was considered very good by the Russians (at least at the altitudes where they customarily fought), and they considered the *Kobra's* horizontal turning radius to be superior to their opponents. However, there were several problems with the P-39 family.

These predominantly centred around the P-39's Allison V-1710 engine, which was temperamental (the same problem afflicted the P-40) and sometimes failed on landing, or even in combat – its distaste for Russian grades of aviation spirit exacerbated the problems. Oil also tended to pool in the engine after flight, and this would then freeze solid in the cold winter weather. Another problem encountered was the fracturing of the main cannon shaft, which punctured the oil pan and cut vital control cables. These technical maladies were all eventually solved by modifications to the motor introduced by Allison at the factory on later versions.

The aircraft's deadly tendency to go into a flat spin (frequently a temptation for a manoeuvrable fighter) was also quickly recognised by the Russians. As there was no technical solution to this problem, pilots had to be taught how to avoid this happening. Nevertheless, a number of Soviet test pilots, as well as frontline types, were killed in spinning accidents.

The final major flaw in the P-39's design only arose should the pilot wish to bail out. As the Americans had discovered within weeks of the fighter entering service, exiting via the side 'car door' was a risky business. Too many Soviet pilots were killed or injured by striking the horizontal tailplane once they had dived out the cockpit – high-scoring aces Nikolai Iskrin and Boris Glinka were both injured in this way, with the latter pilot breaking a collarbone and both legs so severely that he was unable to return to his unit for the last ten months of the war. Pilots were told to bail out only as a last resort. However, they were also told that the P-39's streamlined cowl and low-set wings seemed almost designed for wheels-up landings, and that nobody ever came to grief belly-landing a *Kobra*.

On 15 May 1942 Maj G A Reifshneider's 19 GIAP (manned by 22 pilots, flying 16 Airacobra Is and 10 P-40Es) returned to the front at Shongui, the unit having been strengthened through the addition of a third squadron. That evening the unit flew its first mission with the aircraft, and during the course of the sortie four Airacobras encountered 12 Bf 109s and eight Bf 110s near Lake Tulp-Yavr. Capt Kutakhov and Sr Lt Bochkov each downed a fighter to register the *Kobra's* first kills in Russia.

The next day Bochkov scored again, although 16 May also saw the regiment suffer its first combat loss when Sr Lt Ivan Gaidaenko force-landed Airacobra I AH660 in a forest. The aeroplane was completely torn apart in the landing, although the pilot emerged from the wreckage uninjured, having been protected by the fighter's sturdy construction.

The *Kobra's* first big victory came on 15 June when six fighters intercepted six Ju 88s escorted by 16 Bf 110s heading for Murmansk. Nine German aircraft were claimed to have been shot down for no losses, with Ivan Bochkov being credited with the destruction of a Bf 110 and a Ju 88.

Bochkov would not score again until 10 December, when he led six *Kobras* against a formation of 18 Ju 87s and 12 Bf 109s. It was Soviet policy to always focus on the lead bomber in a formation, so Bochkov ignored the fighters and led his flight in a head-on attack on the Ju 87s. In the first attack two Stukas were downed, including the leader, and the formation disintegrated before the escorts could intervene. Three more aircraft were destroyed during a short turning battle prior to the P-39s disengaging without loss. Bochkov claimed one kill.

By February 1943, when he was nominated for the Hero of the Soviet Union (HSU), Bochkov had completed 308 sorties and scored 7 individual and 32 group victories.

On 4 April, during his 350th mission, Bochkov and his

While this photo is usually identified as showing Ivan Bochkov of 19 GIAP in front of his Airacobra I, the fact that the aircraft carries Bort number 16 raises doubts that this is actually the HSU winner. Indeed, this aircraft was usually flown by fellow 19 GIAP ace Efim Krivosheev, who could very well be the pilot in the photograph. With both men dying relatively early in the Patriotic War, no other photographs exist of either individual to help confirm the identity of this pilot (*via Petrov*)

wingman engaged six Bf 109s. His wingman's aircraft was soon badly damaged, but Bochkov fought on so that his comrade could escape. The ace downed his eighth victory before being shot down and killed.

Seven months earlier, on 9 September 1942, 19 GIAP's Sr Lt Efim Krivosheev had exhibited similar bravery when he had carried out the P-39's first *taran* (ramming) attack.

Such an action was deliberately planned by the pilot usually after he/she had exhausted all ammunition. Typically, only the propeller blades or wingtips would be used in a *taran* attack, the pilot trying to immobilise the enemy's control surfaces. Full collisions often occurred, however.

On this occasion Krivosheev, who had previously scored 5 individual and 15 shared victories, shot down a Bf 109 and then saw his squadron commander, Capt Kutakhov, being attacked by another German fighter. Having exhausted his ammunition, Krivosheev honoured the VVS creed '*tovarishcha vyruchai, a sam pogibai*' ('Protect your buddy, even if you die') and smashed his own aircraft into the German fighter, losing his life in the process. He received a posthumous HSU on 22 February 1943.

Kutakhov finished the war as a colonel, commanding 19 GIAP. He flew 367 sorties and fought 79 aerial combats, and was credited with 13 individual and 28 group victories (although a Soviet historian who recently examined German loss records states that only five of the individual kills can be confirmed). In 1969 he became the Commander in Chief of the Soviet Air Forces, a position he held for 15 years.

Another 19 GIAP pilot with a future was Grigorii Dmitryuk, who joined the regiment as fresh from training in May, just as the first Airacobra Is were being delivered – he initially flew the Kittyhawk, however, before switching to the *Kobra*. By November 1944 he had been promoted to captain and given command of one of the regiment's units. By war's end he had flown 206 sorties, fought 37 combats, scored 18 kills and received the HSU. Dmitryuk also achieved ace status flying MiG-15s over Korea in 1952-53, claiming exactly five kills.

Other units which flew the Airacobra in the north from mid-1943 to the end of the war were the 20 GIAP (serving in Karelia alongside 19 GIAP), all five fighter regiments of the Northern Fleet Air Arm, 102 and 103 GIAPs of the Leningrad PVO District and 191 IAP, which flew over southern Finland.

All these units fought an unsung war in a theatre where there were few dramatic operations, and where adverse weather conditions often posed a greater danger than enemy fighters.

Pavel Klimov of 2 GIAP-SF (Northern Fleet Air Arm) pauses for the camera on the wing of his P-39D just prior to climbing into the cockpit. His regiment, named after its famous commander Boris Safonov, had been the first Soviet unit to fly the Hurricane, and then the P-40. Pavel Klimov was awarded the HSU in August 1943, by which time he had scored 11 individual and 16 shared victories during the course of 306 sorties. Some of his kills were claimed whilst flying the Hurricane (*via Petrov*)

The uniforms worn by these unidentified pilots suggest that they belong to the naval air arm. Note also that the sea eagle insignia that adorns this P-39 is identical to the emblem painted on the side of Pavel Klimov's Airacobra above. Perhaps one of these pilots is Klimov himself? (*via Petrov*)

P-39D SHINES IN THE CAUCASUS

Just as for the British the Spitfire and the Battle of Britain will always be inextricably linked, or for the Americans the Wildcat with the Battle of Midway, for the Russians the Airacobra will always be associated with the battle for the Kuban in the spring and summer of 1943. Though dwarfed by Field Marshal Erich von Manstein's Spring offensive and the Battle of Kursk, it was the campaign over the Blue Line and the Kuban which pitted the best of the Luftwaffe against their counterparts in the Red Air Force. And the best of the Soviet units were the Airacobra regiments, mainly assigned to 216 Air Division, which became the famous 9 Guards Air Division, and which contained many of Russia's most famous fighter pilots.

The division was equipped with P-39D-2s that had arrived in the Soviet Union via the southern route through Iran – once in the USSR, the fighters were issued to regiments flying in the North Caucasus. The route through Iran was chosen in spite of its greater distance because of the losses suffered by the Arctic convoys that had delivered Airacobra Is via Murmansk.

It was also necessary to set up an infrastructure for receiving and assembling the aircraft in Iran, and then ferrying them to the Soviet Union. The first Hurricanes, Kitty-hawks and Bostons began arriving only in June 1942, followed by P-39Ds in September. Upon arrival they were assembled at the port of Abadan and ferried to Azerbaijan, where they were issued to 25 ZAP.

The first three units trained by 25 ZAP were ultimately combined within 9 GIAD. By war's end this air division had been acknowledged as the most formidable in the VVS, its pilots scoring 1147 aerial victories and being awarded with 31 HSUs, including three who won the award twice and one who was so

It has not yet been possible to identify this pilot with certainty, although judging by the 16 stars on the P-39D behind him, he was almost certainly an ace. The single silhouette to the left of the stars supposedly represents an enemy aircraft forced down and captured (*via Petrov*)

Another pair of anonymous P-39 pilots seen in mid 1943. Could this be an ace and his wingman discussing their plans before their next mission? (*via Petrov*)

honoured three times. 298 IAP was the first regiment to receive the P-39D, followed closely by 45 IAP and 16 GIAP.

298 IAP had fought on the Southern Front since the start of the war, firstly with I-153s and I-16s and then with the Yak-1. In January 1943 the regiment was withdrawn from the front to reform with replacement pilots and new aircraft, during which time it gained a third squadron. The unit received 21 P-39D-2s fitted with 20 mm cannon and 11 P-39K-1s boasting the heavier 37 mm weapon. The latter fighters were assigned to the Regiment Commander, the Regiment Navigator, the Deputy Commander/Chief of Aerial Gunnery Service, all three Unit Commanders, and the Regiment and Squadron Deputy Commanders for Political Affairs (the *zampolity*). The flight commanders and regular pilots made do with the P-39Ds.

Commanded by Lt Col Ivan Taranenko, the unit deployed to Korenovskaya airbase on 17 March 1943, where it was assigned to 219 BAD in order to provide fighter escort for its Pe-2s. 298 IAP flew its first sortie almost immediately upon arrival, and suffered its first loss on 19 March when Sgt Belyakov was shot down and killed in P-39D-1 41-38444.

Between 17 March and 20 August the regiment fought some of the hardest aerial battles of the war against the Luftwaffe's 8 *Fliegerkorps* above the Kuban and the Blue Line. During those five months, the regiment flew 1625 sorties and participated in 111 air combats, shooting down 167 enemy aircraft and damaging 29. Its own losses amounted to 30 aircraft shot down and 11 so badly damaged that they needed major repairs.

For this performance, 298 IAP was honoured with the redesignation 104 GIAP on 25 August 1943 and reassigned to 9 GIAD, which was being organised as an elite division around 16 GIAP. Its CO, Lt Col Ivan Taranenko, had scored four individual and four shared victories during this period, and in mid July he was promoted to colonel and assigned to Yak-equipped 294 IAD as its CO. Awarded the HSU on 2 September for his leadership of 298 IAP, Taranenko had increased his score to 16 individual and 4 shared victories by war's end.

Taranenko's successor was Maj Vladimir Semenishin, who had first seen combat over Finland in 1939. He had flown I-16s with 131 IAP from June 1941 until 11 May 1942, when he was badly wounded while flying over the Kuban – barely able to make it back to his base,

Semenishin spent many months recuperating. Once declared fit for flying, he was sent to 25 ZAP and then assigned to 298 IAP as Regimental Navigator, being simultaneously promoted to major.

By May 1943 Semenishin had flown 136 missions and participated in 29 aerial combats, scoring eight individual and seven shared victories. He was awarded the HSU on the 24th of that month, and he celebrated three days later by claiming four kills in two sorties. On 18 July he succeeded Lt Col I A Taranenko as commander of the regiment, and soon after he was promoted to lieutenant-colonel. Semenishin was a popular leader, possessing the mind of a tactician and the tutoring skills of a teacher.

Vladimir Semenishin's tenure as CO of 104 GIAP was to last until 29 September 1943. On this day he was leading a flight of nine P-39s that became separated near the frontline in bad weather. Semenishin and his two wingmen continued on until they were 'bounced' by nine Bf 109s, which downed one of the *Kobras* before the Soviet pilots could react. The ace countered by turning into his foes and launching a ferocious attack, destroying three Bf 109s before being killed. His final score was 23 individual and 13 shared victories during the course of 300+ missions.

Another of 298 IAP's outstanding pilots was Mikhail Komel'kov, who had seen action from the first day of the war until he was wounded in October 1941. Upon his release from hospital, he was assigned as an instructor to 25 ZAP rather than returning to the front. During his service with the unit Komel'kov trained 171 fighter pilots, initially on the LaGG-3 and MiG-3, before moving onto the P-39 in late 1942.

Anxious to get to the front, he managed to have himself reassigned as a replacement pilot and returned to combat with 298 IAP in March 1943. The regiment soon felt the benefit of his arrival, for on 16 April Komel'kov scored three victories in three sorties – his final tally for the Kuban campaign totalled 15 kills. Promoted to captain and made a squadron leader, Komel'kov had become deputy commander of the regiment, with the rank of major, by the end of the war. Completing 321 sorties, he participated in 75 combats and scored 32 individual and 7 shared victories. Komel'kov was awarded the HSU on 27 June 1945.

Among the seasoned members of 298 IAP was Vasilii Drygin, who had joined the regiment in June 1942 from 4 IAP. Surviving the fighting retreat, he transitioned to the P-39 with the regiment's few remaining original pilots, and then returned to the action in 1943. Drygin was particularly prolific during the fighting over the Blue line, where he scored ten individual and five shared kills.

Two of these victories were scored on 2 May, whilst flying as part of a foursome with Maj Semenishin. Encountering a dozen Ju 87s with a fighter escort, Drygin and his wingman went after the dive-bombers, despatching two and one respectively. Then, having disrupted the bombing attack, he rushed to the aid of Maj Semenishin, who was holding off the escorts. In the resulting melee, Drygin bailed out of his blazing fighter, although he was back in the air again the very next day. Indeed, within 24 hours of the incident, he had helped Maj Semenishin and another pilot force an undamaged Bf 109 to land at their airfield.

Drygin was awarded the HSU on 24 May 1943, by which time he had completed 261 missions and tackled with the Luftwaffe on 40 separate occasions. Although he had downed 12 aircraft individually and shared in the destruction of five others, Drygin was far from finished, and on 7 June he destroyed three Bf 109s in a day. By war's end his score had risen to 20.

Another 'old-timer' was Konstantin Vishnevetskii, who began the war with 298 IAP in 1941. In the frontline at the time of the invasion of eastern Poland in September 1939, he had found no aerial opposition during the latter campaign. Come June 1941 Vishnevetskii was already a senior lieutenant leading one of 298 IAP's units, and having survived the battles of 1941-42, he converted onto the P-39. With 123 missions behind him by September 1943, his score stood at 10 individual and 13 shared kills.

Vishnevetskii was badly wounded in an engagement over the Blue Line during this period, yet he managed to return his aircraft to base and land in spite of copious blood loss. He was awarded the HSU on 24 August 1943, and promoted to major shortly afterward. The following month Vishnevetskii claimed two kills during a dogfight over the Molochnaya River, but he was again wounded in the process and forced to limp home. His right arm was so badly injured on this occasion that it was rendered partially useless, and he was removed from flight duty. Vishnevetskii had by then flown 200 sorties and scored 20 individual and 15 shared victories. He was killed in a traffic accident on 30 July 1944.

The second regiment to convert to the P-39D was 45 IAP, which had fought across the Crimea and northern Caucasus from the beginning of 1942 under the leadership of Lt Col Ibragim Magometovich Dzusov – although barely an ace himself, he was one of the VVS's outstanding leaders of aces. Born an Ossetian (one of the Muslim minority peoples of the Caucasus) in 1905, he was already a Red Army soldier prior to his 15th birthday, fighting the anti-Communist Basmachi in Soviet Central Asia.

In 1929 Dzusov completed flight school and committed himself to a career in the VVS. When he led 45 IAP to the front in January 1942 he was already 37 years old, and trying to survive in an era when fighter combat was very much a young man's game. And although he failed to achieve the high scores of his contemporaries, Dzusov was both liked and respected by his pilots, and he knew how to organise and lead. On 16 June 1943 he left 45 IAP to take command of 9 GIAD, where he

An anonymous Guards Regiment P-39D. While the location of the aircraft number on the nose and the Guards badge on the cockpit door establish that this is not a *Kobra* of any of the regiments of 9 GIAD, or of several other units, there are still a number of possible regiments to which it might belong (*Russian Aviation Research Trust*)

remained until May 1944, when he was appointed overall commander of 6 YAK. In spite of his command responsibilities, and his age, Maj-Gen Dzusov flew 89 missions and scored six kills in 11 combats, though it is uncertain how many of these may have been scored in the *Kobra*.

Although Dzusov's 45 IAP had arrived at 25 ZAP in late October 1942 – a full two-and-a-half months before 298 IAP – its conversion proved to be more complicated, and they ended up going into action within days of each other. 45 IAP initially converted onto the P-40, spending time practicing combat flying and training pilots newly-arrived from flight school.

Just as the unit was on the verge of returning to the frontline with its P-40s, the first *Kobras* arrived. The decision was quickly made to reorganise the regiment into three squadrons, which were staffed by 31 pilots in total, and issued with sufficient aircraft to equip two units with P-39s and one with the P-40. This took still more time to achieve, and it was not until early March 1943 that 45 IAP was ready to join 216 SAD at the front. When it departed, the 1st and 3rd squadrons had 10 P-39Ds and 11 P-39Ks respectively, whilst the 2nd squadron had 10 P-40Es.

On 9 March 45 IAP deployed to the airfield at Krasnodar, and it immediately entered battle, losing its first P-39D (41-38433) the following day. Twenty-four hours later two more *Kobras* were damaged seriously enough to need repairs. Thus, although 45 IAP had been the second regiment to receive the P-39 in the North Caucasus, and had spent far longer in training, it was still the first to take it into combat.

22 March saw eight *Kobras* of 45 IAP fight a difficult battle against a formation of 30 Bf 109Gs, and although the Soviets claimed 13 Messerschmitts destroyed, they suffered the loss of three aircraft. Two pilots died executing *taran* attacks in their burning P-39s, namely Sgt N Kudryashov and Sr Lt Ivan Shmatko, the latter pilot having scored eight victories flying Yaks with the regiment during the summer of 1942. In another battle that same day, future P-39 ace Boris Glinka was wounded by the rear gunner of a Ju 87, although he returned to action almost immediately.

Boris Borisovich Glinka and and his brother Dmitrii Borisovich both served in 45 IAP/100 GIAP and both became leading Soviet aces. Boris was the older, and had finished his flying training in 1940. Boris was serving as a lieutenant with 45 IAP when the war broke out, but in spite of seeing much action, he did not manage to score any victories in 1942 – only when he came to the *Kobra* did he find his weapon. Awarded the HSU on 24 May 1943 after scoring ten kills in March and April, Boris would eventually claim 30 victories. In the summer of 1944 he was transferred to 16 GIAP as the commander of that famous regiment.

Despite being three years younger than Boris, Dmitrii Glinka joined the army first and duly completed his flying training ahead of his older brother. He was also assigned to 45 IAP, but as a senior lieutenant and deputy commander for aerial gunnery. Dmitrii also managed to score six kills while flying the Yak-1 in the spring of 1942, although he was also shot down and wounded, spending two months in hospital.

By the middle of April 1943 Dmitrii Glinka had completed his 146th sortie and scored his 15th victory. On the 15th of that month the regiment experienced one of its worst days, and he was one of four pilots shot down – Dmitrii had destroyed two Ju 88s prior to his demise, however. Wounded once again, and forced to take to his parachute, he spent a week

This P-39 features a style of numbering similar to that seen on the fighter on page 58. Notice, however, that there is no Guards badge on the cockpit door, nor on any of the pilots' uniforms. Therefore, this is almost certainly a different unidentified regiment (*Russian Aviation Research Trust*)

in hospital recuperating, and then returned to action with his arm still in a splint. Within hours of Glinka returning to his regiment, two more P-39s (flown by Sr Lt Petrov and Sgt Bezbabnov) were shot down, one of them being future ranking German ace Erich Hartmann's seventh kill. That same day Glinka received the HSU for his first 15 victories.

On 30 April Dmitrii managed to destroy three Ju 87s in a single sortie. Then on 4 May, during an attack on the airfield at Sarabuz that had seen him destroy a Bf 109 on the ground, he spotted an unlucky Ju 52/3m that had arrived over the airstrip just as it was being strafed. Dmitrii quickly shot it down. In the early summer (probably at about the same time as 45 IAP became the 100 GIAP) Dmitrii Glinka was promoted to captain, and on 24 August he became a two-time HSU winner for completing 186 sorties and scoring 29 kills.

In September Glinka had another close call, although this incident could have been totally avoidable. He was examining a captured German hand grenade when it exploded, although fortunately for him it only caused minor wounds to his legs. Within days, he was back in the air, and had scored eight more victories by the beginning of December when 9 GIAD was withdrawn for a rest. Dmitrii returned to the front in May 1944, taking part in the Jassy-Kishinev operation. During the first week of the campaign, he shot down another six aircraft, including three Ju 87s in a single mission at the beginning of the month. He then had yet another close escape, although this time it was not his fault.

Dmitrii was a passenger in an Li-2 transport which became lost in bad weather and crashed into a mountain. Seriously injured, the ace lay in the wreckage for a whole two days before being rescued, and he was subsequently off operations for a full two months. Promoted to major upon his return, Glinka participated in the Lvov-Sandomir operation, during which he added another nine kills to his score. He then participated in the Berlin operation, scoring three victories in a day, before claiming his final kill on 18 April 1945 when he downed a Fw 190 in an engagement fought at a height of just 30 metres. His final wartime tally of 50 victories was scored during the course of 300 sorties and 90 combats.

Another 100 GIAP pilot to distinguish himself over the Kuban was former chemistry and mathematics teacher Ivan Babak. He had joined the army in 1940, and was still undergoing training when the Germans invaded. Rushed through the remainder of his course, and graduating in April 1942, Babak was immediately sent off to Yak-1-equipped 45 IAP. He initially failed to impress his regiment commander, Lt Col Dzusov, who was ready to send him away, but ace D L Kalarash took him under his wing and helped him adjust to frontline flying. With his rehabilitation completed, Babak was asked by Dmitrii Glinka to fly as his wingman.

He scored his first victory over Mozdok in September, and when 45 IAP returned to the front in March, Babak added more kills to his tally by shooting down a Bf 109 and a Ju 87. In April 1943 he was credited with 14 fighters destroyed over the Kuban, singling Babak out as one of the leading *Kobra* aces, the peer of Fadeev, Pokryshin and his mentor, Dmitrii Glinka. However, just as he was reaching the peak of his success, Babak contracted malaria, which put him in hospital until September.

Upon his return to 100 GIAP Babak was given a new P-39N, and on his first sortie with the aircraft he shot another Bf 109 down. Awarded the HSU on 1 November 1943, he was soon back in the hospital, however, following a recurrence of his malaria. Kept out of the action until well into 1944, Babak returned to his unit (as 100 GIAP's deputy commander for aerial weaponry) on the eve of the Jassy-Kishinev operation.

Proving that his ability as a fighter pilot was undiminished by his bouts of illness, Babak destroyed four Fw 190s in a single mission on 16 July whilst flying in support of the Lvov-Sandomir operation. He was posted to 16 GIAP as regimental commander in March 1945, and his veteran P-39N was passed on to fellow ace Grigorii Dol'nikov.

Another veteran ace from 45 IAP was Nikolai Lavitskii, who had joined the regiment in 1941 and downed his first kill (a Bf 109) flying an I-153. By the time 45 IAP withdrew to re-equip with the P-39, he had flown 186 sorties and scored 11 individual and 1 shared victories. During the summer of 1943 Lavitskii scored four more kills with the P-39, and on 24 August was awarded the HSU – he was also promoted to captain and placed in charge of the 3rd squadron.

Despite his success as a fighter pilot, Lavitskii's personal life was in turmoil, and his wife divorced him whilst he was at the front. From then on he volunteered for every mission, particularly the most hazardous ones. His bravery turned into recklessness, seriously worrying his friends, who felt he had a death wish. Lavitskii continued on his path to self-destruction despite I M Dzusov becoming CO of 9 GIAD, and moving him to division headquarters as deputy division commander for air gunnery. The ace finally found the death he had sought for so long during a training flight on 10 March 1944, by which time he had had flown 250+ sorties and been credited with 24 individual and 2 shared kills.

In the spring of 1943 a reform of VVS policy changed the practice of allowing regiments to exhaust themselves in the frontline, and providing replacements only in the rear ZAPs. From this point on, aircraft and ZAP-trained pilots would be sent to regiments still fighting at the front. Two such individuals who joined 100 GIAP in the summer of 1943 were future aces Pyotr Guchyok and Grigorii Dol'nikov. Guchyok arrived in August 1943, and soon became Ivan Babak's wingman. He remained in

This P-39N-0 (42-4983) shows no signs of the blue background circle underneath the red star, nor of overpainting, and the yellow serial number remains intact on the tail. A careful look will reveal that the background aircraft has its Bort number ('White 48') applied in a fatter style than the thin '43' of the closest aircraft. Sadly, the unit flying these fighters again remains unidentifiable (*via Petrov*)

the frontline until lost to flak on 18 April 1945, by which time he had flown 209 sorties and scored 18 individual and 3 shared victories.

Grigorii Dol'nikov had joined 100 GIAP fresh from completing his flying training, and he was assigned to Dmitrii Glinka as his wingman. On 30 September he claimed his first kills when he destroyed two Ju 87s, although he in turn was shot down and captured. Dol'nikov remained incarcerated until 2 December, when he succeeded in escaping from German captivity back to Soviet lines thanks to the help of Russian partisans.

His ordeal did not end there, however, for Stalin's Order No 227 had declared that being taken prisoner constituted treason, regardless of the circumstances! Although this rule was not always enforced, serious unpleasantness awaited all escaping PoWs, who had to endure an extended interrogation and investigation by SMERSh (military police), before being permitted to 'return to duty' – the latter often meant assignment to a penal battalion, or occasionally a labour camp instead of the frontline. Dol'nikov was eventually cleared and allowed to return to his regiment, but not until May 1944. By war's end he had flown 160 sorties and scored 15 individual and 1 shared victories.

The third regiment to take the P-39D into action over the Blue line was not only the most famous of all *Kobra* units, but possibly the most renowned regiment in the history of Russian airpower – 16 GIAP. While this regiment was only the second highest scoring (697 victories) IAP in the Soviet Air Forces, it had the largest number of heroes (15 HSUs), including two pilots who received the award twice, and one of only two three-time winners in the Soviet Air Forces. Indeed, only three individuals won it three times in the entire armed forces – Marshal G K Zhukov received his third HSU in 1945, and a unique fourth in 1956.

Designated 55 IAP when war broke out, the unit (commanded by Maj V P Ivanov) was in the process of converting from I-153s and I-16s to the MiG-3 at Beltsy, on the Romanian border. Amongst its crop of pilots was a Snr Lt Aleksandr Pokryshkin, who got off to a bad start on day one of the invasion when he shot down a Su-2 bomber which he had failed to recognise as Soviet – he was able to score his first legitimate victory 24 hours later. 55 IAP flew mainly reconnaissance and ground attack missions during 1941, and it was redesignated 16 GIAP on 7 March 1942.

By the end of the year Pokryshkin had completed 316 sorties, scored four victories and been shot down by flak once during a reconnaissance mission, landing behind German lines but evading capture. This did not seem a good harbinger of his future success, although the best evidence of Pokryshkin's skill may have been his very survival. During this dark period he began laying the ground work for his later success, and also the success of the Soviet Air Force – he spent much time studying his regiment's air encounters, and analysing its tactics.

Like other Soviet aces who were doing the same thing, and coming independently to similar conclusions, Pokryshkin decided that both the air force's equipment and tactics were inferior to the enemy's. He soon found himself officially in trouble for criticising Soviet fighter designs, and Pokryshkin's outspoken views may have also been the source of the difficulties which developed between him and the regimental navigator.

During the spring of 1942 16 GIAP was able to dispense with the last of its I-153s and I-16s when further Yak-1s were received, although it was

A young Aleksandr Pokryshkin prepares to climb into his MiG-3 (out of shot) in late 1941. Pokryshkin was one of the relatively few pilots able to get good results from this 'difficult' aircraft, and he had earned his first Hero award before converting onto the P-39D. He found scoring much easier with the American fighter (*via Petrov*)

still stuck with the obsolete MiG-3. Now flying the Yakovlev fighter, Pokryshkin began to increase his score, and at the end of 1942 his tally stood at 12 kills (including eight Bf 109s) from 354 sorties.

In early January 1943 16 GIAP was sent to 25 ZAP for an infusion of new pilots and re-equipment with the P-39, both of which allowed it to form a larger three-squadron regiment – the unit received 14 P-39L-1s, 7 P-39K-1s and 11 P-39D-2s. On 8 April 16 GIAP returned to the front at Krasnodar, assigned to 216 SAD, and began operations the next day.

During April the regiment flew 289 sorties with the P-39 and 13 with the P-40E, and was credited with 79 victories – 14 Bf 109Es, 12 Bf 109Fs, 45 Bf 109Gs, 2 Fw 190As, 4 Ju 88As, 1 Do 217 and 1 Ju 87D (these aircraft types were identified by reading engine number plates or other data whilst inspecting the remains of shot down aircraft).

In return, 16 GIAP lost 19 P-39s in combat and two in accidents, along with 11 pilots, and received 19 P-39s and four P-40Es as replacements. By 1 June, its strength had again been reduced to 19 P-39s, the regiment's overall loss of 36 fighters being evidence of the fierceness of the air battles.

During April Pokryshkin was credited with ten Bf 109s and Grigorii Rechkalov seven Messerschmitt fighters and a Ju-88. Outscoring both, however, was Vadim Fadeev, who claimed 12 Bf 109s destroyed.

On Pokryshkin's first combat mission in the P-39, on 9 April, he and Rechkalov were both credited with Bf 109s shot down. Three days later Pokryshkin scored a double and Rechkalov scored again too – the former had actually claimed seven kills on 12 April, but he was only able to gain confirmation for two of them. He claimed further victories on the 15th, 16th and 20th, and on the 29th succeeded in shooting down four Bf 109s in a single sortie. Pokryshkin was awarded the HSU on 24 April and exchanged his old P-39D-2 'White 13' for new N-model (the famous 'White 100'), which he flew for the rest of the war. He was promoted to major the following month, having been CO of his unit since early 1943.

And just as things were going well for the ace, his career was almost terminated by the regiment's commander (and former navigator), Zaev. Relations between the two had deteriorated throughout 1942, and in mid-1943 he took measures to have Pokryshkin expelled from the regiment, stripped of his HSU and called before a tribunal. After some considerable difficulty, the regimental *komissar* was able to clear Pokryshkin's name, and reputation, and he was awarded his second HSU, on 24 August, for completing 455 sorties and scoring 30 individual victories.

Undeterred by the political machinations of his CO, Pokryshkin had been busy developing and perfecting his new tactics during the spring and summer of 1943. The old pre-war tactic of flying in formations of threes and sixes, either in line abreast or in a 'V', and then rigidly maintaining formation throughout any aerial battle which ensued had proven obsolete. Seeing the effectiveness of the enemy's open formations, Pokryshkin reduced the size of his squadron's flights to four fighters, which he further split into elements of two. However, he still maintained that the wingman had to be scrupulous in maintaining formation with his leader.

During the summer he introduced the 'Kuban Stairs' tactic, in which the strike flight flying at a lower altitude would be covered by another flight behind it, and at a higher altitude, ready to surprise any enemy fighters that might try to surprise it. And this second flight would in turn

A later photograph of Pokryshkin taken in front of his P-39. The lightweight nature of his uniform suggests that this shot must have been taken during the summer of 1943 – shortly after his conversion onto the P-39 (*via D Maksimov*)

be covered by its own flight higher still. Pokryshkin also came to prefer the diving attack (again a favourite of the Luftwaffe) instead of the classic turning battle or head-on assault. This called for a surprise attack to made from higher altitude, diving at high speed. Once close to the enemy, the pilot would open fire and then dive away. Using the momentum of the dive, he would zoom climb back to a higher altitude and repeat the attack if necessary. Pokryshkin summed this tactic up in his own famous short-hand, *'vysota-skorost-manevr-ogon'* ('height-speed-manoeuvre-fire').

His tactics came to be generally adopted by the Soviet Air Force, and the 'Kuban Stairs' still proved successful for the Soviet-trained North Vietnamese Peoples' Air Force during the Vietnam War. Pokryshkin also developed the practice of 'free hunting', in which 16 GIAP pilots were allowed to execute fighter sweeps, looking for combat rather than being tasked with close bomber escort or air cover duties typical of Red Air Force fighter missions until then. This in turn gave pilots the chance to struggle for an initiative previously denied them by their own tactics.

Toward the end of 1943 Pokryshkin attended an 8th Air Army-sponsored conference concerned with the wider development and use of free hunting, and this tactic gradually became popular throughout much of the Soviet Air Force. Several elite IAPs were tasked mainly with free hunting, whilst most IADs and IAKs established 'Sword Flights' composed of their best pilots, freed of routine assignments and given hunting duties.

For Pokryshkin, one negative feature of the new tactic was that he was no longer able to get confirmation for all of his victories – he claimed 13 kills which could not be confirmed or included in his score.

After clearing the Kuban, Pokryshkin's air division led the way in the battle to liberate the southern Ukraine, his pilots particularly distinguishing themselves in the September battle for the Donbas region and the liberation of Mariupol. At the end of 1943 16 GIAP and 9 GIAD were withdrawn into reserve for a period of rest and reconstitution.

The great rival to 'Sasha' Pokryshkin, the top-scoring Airacobra pilot, and the third-ranking Allied ace was Grigorii 'Grisha' Rechkalov, whom doctors repeatedly forbade to fly! After joining the military and completing his training, Rechkalov was excluded from flying by a medical board because of his colour blindness and farsightedness. However, with the approach of war in 1941, such vision questions suddenly seemed less important, and in June he found himself flying I-153s and I-16s on the Southwestern Front. Rechkalov scored two kills, but he was also shot down and forced to endure three operations and several months in hospital, where doctors again forbade him from returning to the air.

Numerous appeals, severe Soviet losses and some flying demonstrations by Rechkalov himself eventually saw him return to the front in the summer of 1942 when he was assigned to 16 GIAP. He scored a few more victories with the

A proud declaration by the Allies' third ranking ace, Capt Grigorii Rechkalov. His fighter shows only his 56 individual victories, and omits his six shared kills, which had previously been displayed on this P-39 (*Russian Aviation Research Trust*)

Yak-1, but only truly found his mark in April 1943 when the regiment returned to the front with the P-39. Along with Pokryshkin, he shot down a Bf 109 during 16 GIAP's first *Kobra* sortie on 9 April, and by month-end he had scored eight victories, and been promoted to senior lieutenant.

On 24 May Rechkalov received the HSU for 194 sorties and 12 individual and 2 shared kills, and in June he became commander of 16 GIAP's 1st squadron. Claiming two Ju 52/3ms and a Romanian Savoia Z.501 flying boat over the Black Sea during the autumn of 1943, Rechkalov continued his scoring run into 1944.

Sharing the limelight at 16 GIAP in 1943 with the likes of Rechkalov and Pokryshkin was Vadim Fadeev, who at the time challenged, and even exceeded, the accomplishments of his fellow aces. He was known across the front as *Boroda* ('The Beard'), a nickname he himself used on the radio – the source of this name was his long, uncut chin whiskers. He had begun the war as a senior sergeant flying the I-16 on the Southern Front, and he quickly distinguished himself by his exceptionally bold strafing attacks, which saw him fly lower than anyone else.

It was during the course of one such attack, on a German artillery position during the battle for Rostov-on-Don in November 1941, that the engine in Fadeev's fighter was damaged by the shrapnel from an exploding ammunition dump. Turning for home, he belly-landed his I-16 in no-man's land. With bullets flying all around him, Fadeev jumped from the cockpit and sprinted to the closest Soviet trench, where he immediately relayed his latest reconnaissance and target information to a senior army officer. The latter in turn targeted Soviet artillery on the German artillery emplacement. Fadeev also recommended an immediate Soviet counter-attack, and when the infantry left their trenches he unholstered his pistol and led the assault!

In December 1941 he was transferred to 630 IAP, equipped with Kittyhawks, and in January 1942 he claimed his first kill, followed by five more by year-end. Late in the 1942 Fadeev was posted to 16 GIAP.

The ace soon became a favourite not only with his regiment, but along the entire Soviet front, his skill and boldness, and his good nature, becoming legendary. By the end of April 1943 Fadeev had been promoted to captain and made CO of 16 GIAP's 3rd squadron. He had flown 394 missions and scored 17 individual and 3 group kills in 43 combats.

The seemingly indestructible Vadim Fadeev was killed in combat on 5 May 1943 when his flight of six P-39s was ambushed by a group of eight Bf 109s. Four of the German fighters singled out the Russian ace's P-39, and despite Fadeev's attempt to counter their attacks with a head-on pass, he was boxed in from all sides and his aircraft was hit by a burst of fire, wounding him in the side – the *Kobra's* engine was also badly damaged. Weak from massive blood loss, Fadeev managed to belly land on the steppe,

Fellow aces Andrei Trud and Vadim Fadeev of 16 GIAP sit on the wing of the latter's P-39D-2. Fadeev is holding the leather case which Soviet pilots used for carrying their maps and other documents. It is easy to see why Fadeev was famed as the 'Beard' (*via D Maksimov*)

Aleksandr Klubov was one of the star pilots of 16 GIAP, this formal photo being taken soon after he had received his first HSU in April 1944 (*via D Maksimov*)

although he had died in the cockpit of his fighter by the time soldiers reached him. He was posthumously awarded the HSU on 24 May.

Arriving at 16 GIAP just weeks prior to Vadim Fadeev's demise was Aleksandr Klubov, who would ultimately achieve even more victories than the bearded ace. Although he had graduated from flight school in 1940, Klubov was not sent to the front until August 1942 – and then to a regiment still flying old I-153s. During the course of 150 sorties he destroyed six aircraft on the ground and four in the air, before being shot down in flames over Mozdok on 2 November 1942. Klubov successfully bailed out, although he was badly burned and had to spend months in hospital – his face bore the scars of this incident for the rest of his life.

When Klubov returned to duty, he was promoted to captain and assigned to 16 GIAP as a deputy squadron commander. He soon made an impression. One notable fight took place on 15 August 1943 when his flight of six P-39s found two Fw 189 *Ramas* (*Rama* is Russian for window frame, which was the pilots' nickname for this most-hated aircraft) with four Bf 109 escorts. Splitting his forces to attack from both sides, Klubov and his pilots downed both *Ramas* for no losses. By the beginning of September 1943 Aleksandr Klubov had flown 310 sorties and scored 14 individual and 19 shared kills. He received the HSU on 13 April 1944.

In the spring of 1944 Klubov was appointed commander of the 3rd squadron, and later that year he was also named regimental deputy commander for air gunnery. One of his notable air combats came on 29 May when his formation of eight P-39s led an attack on a formation of Ju 88s. In their initial attack Klubov's group shot down two bombers, and then, when the escort intervened, the ace destroyed a Bf 109. The next day his flight met nine Ju 87s escorted by ten Bf 109s, and Klubov downed the leader of the Stuka formation, thus disrupting the attack. His own aircraft was damaged by one of the Bf 109s, however, and he only just made it back to base. During the subsequent fighting of the Jassy-Kishinev operation, Klubov scored 13 kills in a week, including two Ju 87s on 16 July.

Having survived 457 missions, and scored 31 individual and 19 shared victories, Aleksandr Klubov lost his life in a landing accident while converting from the P-39 to the La-7 on 1 November 1944. He was posthumously awarded a second HSU on 27 June 1945.

Yet another HSU winner to fly with 16 GIAP was Nikolai Iskrin, who was serving with 131 IAP in June 1941. He transferred to 55 IAP in February 1942, and by the end of May 1943 he had been promoted to senior lieutenant, and made deputy commander of the 2nd squadron. Iskrin was awarded the HSU on 24 August 1943, by which time he had flown 218 missions, and scored 10 individual and 1 shared victories in 58 combats.

Shot down and wounded days later, the ace hit the tailplane of his P-39 whilst bailing out and badly broke his left leg. Indeed, the injury was so severe that the limb was later amputated. This did not deter Iskrin, however, who returned to 16 GIAP after being fitted with a prosthesis. He completed a further 79 sorties, and claimed six more individual kills.

Not all of the replacement pilots sent to 16 GIAP in the spring of 1943 had been trained to fly fighters, Pavel Eryomin, for example, having completed many missions in Tupolev SBs and B-25 Mitchells prior to joining the crack regiment. With Pokryshkin's careful tutelage, he learned his new craft well, fighting all the way to Berlin and scoring 22 kills.

Another pilot who benefited from Pokryshkin's attention was Georgii Golubev. Serving as an instructor at the start of the war, Golubev had a frustrating time getting into action, being repeatedly stymied by lack of aircraft or bouts of malaria. And when he finally got into action in mid-1942, he found that his I-153

was so obsolete that he had no hope of shooting anything down. Golubev was eventually sent to 84 IAP (later 101 GIAP), where he converted onto the *Kobra*, but prior to reaching the front, he was again transferred to 16 GIAP in May 1943, and assigned to Fadeev's squadron.

When Golubev was introduced to his mechanic, he noticed an unbelieving look on his face.

'Golubev?'

'Yes, Golubev, Georgii. What is it?'

'Oh nothing really. My pilot before you was also Golubev. Only he was a lieutenant. They shot him down. They say he was experienced, but he never returned.'

'I'll try not to let them shoot me down', replied Golubev.

Golubev was fortunate, for Pokryshkin was famous for training his new pilots in how to fight and survive before leading them into combat. After much practice, the ace decided that his new replacements were ready, and Golubev and one other were selected to join in a *Stormovik* support mission led by Pokryshkin. During the sortie two Bf 109s were downed as they tried to attack the Il-2s. It was a good introduction to aerial combat.

More missions followed, and during one of them Golubev downed a Hs 129 under Pokryshkin's watchful eye. After landing, the ace came over and said 'You're a fellow Siberian, let's fly together'. Golubev had just been asked to take responsibility for flying wing for his country's leading ace! He was overawed, but Pokryshkin reassured him. 'It won't be too hard. You'll learn to predict all my thoughts, and I'll learn to guess yours'.

Soon after, on one of their first flights together, they intercepted a Fw 189 *Rama*. Pokryshkin attacked, and when the *Rama* manoeuvred to escape, he chased it into a position where Golubev could shoot it down. In his earphones Golubev heard, 'Excellent Zhora, you read my thoughts'. On a number of occasions, Pokryshkin allowed Golubev to claim a kill, and on occasion they would trade places in formation.

On one occasion in August 1943, Golubev's P-39 was damaged and began to burn while he was trying to return to base. He bailed out, and as he jumped he began to spin. Knowing this would foul his parachute, Golubev delayed pulling the ripcord and spread his arms and legs to stop the spin. Only then could he pull the cord. The parachute opened just 150 metres above the ground, and Golubev landed among Soviet troops.

Golubev continued to fly wing for Pokryshkin, and they became close on the ground. Eventually, in 1944, when the latter was promoted to command 9 GIAD, Golubev became a pair leader himself, though when Pokryshkin flew with the regiment, he still often selected Golubev as wingman. Golubev eventually scored 12 kills, his last being a Do 217 downed over Prague on the last day of the war.

SOVIET VICTORY IN THE AIR

While the P-39 was most famous for its battles on the two flanks, it also served with distinction on the main fronts. The units primarily involved were 153 and 185 IAPs, which were the first to be trained on the *Kobra* at 22 ZAP. On 29 June 1942 153 IAP, consisting of two squadrons and 20 Airacobras commanded by Maj Sergei Mironov, deployed to the airfield at Voronezh, and flew its first sortie the next day. The unit then relocated to Lipetsk.

Maj Mironov had first seen combat against Finland during the Winter War, flying 37 ground attack sorties in the I-153 and claiming one victory. Awarded the HSU for his efforts, Mironov was serving with 153 IAP by June 1941, and had become regiment commander in early 1942.

Under Mironov's leadership 153 IAP operated on the Voronezh Front for 59 days, flying 1070 sorties. Its pilots claimed 61 kills (39 Bf 109s, 1 Bf 110, 1 Me 210, 1 C 200, 15 Ju 88s, 1 Do 217, 1 He 111, 1 Fw 189 and 1 Hs 126) for the loss of eight aircraft and three pilots in combat and two aircraft and one pilot to non-combat causes. In addition, during August eight aircraft under Maj Rodionov's command had operated independently on the western front, flying an additional 167 sorties and claiming four Bf 109s and nine Ju 88s for the loss of two aircraft, and two pilots wounded in combat, and one aircraft and its pilot to non-combat causes.

On 1 October the regiment was withdrawn to Ivanovo, and 22 ZAP, to replace its losses and restructure under the three-squadron organisation. Maj Mironov was promoted to lieutenant colonel at this time and assigned to the Main Administration of Combat Training, with Maj Rodionov taking his place as CO of 153 IAP. Given command of 193 IAD later in the war, Col Mironov had completed 400+ sorties and scored 17 kills (plus his single victory during the Winter War) by May 1945.

When Axis forces threatened to penetrate Soviet lines on the Northwestern Front in late 1942, 153 IAP was rushed into action before it had completely regrouped. And with the weather worsening, the unit enjoyed just nine days of flying in November. Nevertheless, it completed 94 sorties and claimed four Bf 109s and two Ju 87s for the loss of two P-39s.

On 21 November the regiment was designated 28 GIAP, and its record over the next nine months fully lived up to its newly-awarded guards status. From 1 December 1942 to 1 August 1943 the regiment flew 1176 sorties with the Airacobra I, scoring 63 victories (23 Bf 109s, 23 Fw 190s, 6 Ju 88s, 7 Fw 189s and 4 Hs 126s), as well as four balloons, and seven aircraft damaged, in exchange for 14 aircraft lost in combat, five bombed on the ground and four written off in accidents, and the loss of ten pilots. In August the regiment was re-equipped with P-39N/Qs.

With a record of 140 victories for the loss of just 24 P-39s and 13 pilots killed, it is surprising that none of 28 GIAP's aces became famous.

Fellow *Kobra* pioneers 185 IAP, commanded by Lt Col Vasin, went to 22 ZAP following operations on the Leningrad and Volkhov Fronts. Arriving at the unit at about the same time as 153 IAP, it left for the front just one day later. Almost nothing is known about its subsequent combat history, save that the unit was disbanded in August 1942 and its pilots assigned to ferry regiments flying P-39s from Alaska across Siberia. This secretive lack of noted achievement suggests that 185 IAP may have performed badly at the front, suffering serious losses without victories.

Another unit which seems to have failed with the *Kobra* was 494 IAP. It had flown native Russian fighters on the Southern Front during 1942, and in March 1943 was sent to 25 ZAP, where it converted to the P-39D. 494 IAP left for the front in August, and after a brief spell assigned to Stavka reserves, it was assigned to 303 IAD on the Western Front – the division which also contained the French *'Normandie'* regiment.

For some reason the regiment managed to fly only 62 sorties in two months, which breaks down to an average of just one sortie per P-39 per month! Its pilot claimed a mere three kills for the loss of one aircraft and its pilot. In December 1943 494 IAP returned to 25 ZAP, where it was disbanded. This suggests that the low level of activity was due more to regimental deficiencies than to lack of opportunity.

The third regiment to cycle through Airacobra conversion at 22 ZAP was 180 IAP, which arrived in a depleted state on 20 July 1942 – it had only left this unit, equipped with Hurricanes, five weeks earlier. On 3 August the regiment began its conversion, and the process seems to have taken some time for it was held in reserve until 13 March 1943.

On 21 November 1942, whilst still undergoing its conversion training, the unit was redesignated 30 GIAP in recognition of its earlier battles. When it returned to the front in March, its personnel were virtually all new to the regiment, including its CO, Lt Col Khasan Ibatullin. He had previously scored several victories while flying the I-153 and I-16, before being shot down and wounded in July 1942. He remained commander of 30 GIAP until war's end, scoring his last two kills on 18 April 1945 to take his tally to 15 individual victories from 456 sorties.

The real stars of the regiment were Mikhail Petrovich Rents and Aleksandr Petrovich Filatov. Rents had completed flight school at Odessa in 1939 and was sent to the Far East, where he served as an instructor until he was posted to 180 IAP in October 1942. Despite having no combat experience, his many hours spent flying as an instructor gave him a distinct advantage over newer pilots, and he was made a flight commander.

When 30 GIAP returned to combat in March 1943, it was assigned to 1 GIAD of 16 Air Army on the Central Front, based near Kursk. Rents scored his first kill on 22 May, when he led a flight of four P-39s against a large formation of Ju 87s, escorted by Fw 190s. In the first attack he downed a fighter, while the leader of the second pair got a bomber – three more Ju 87s were destroyed before the Germans fled. Five days later Rents was attacked by three Fw 190s, which forced him to bail out of his spinning P-39. He did not score many personal successes during the rest of 1943, and had only three individual kills by the start of 1944.

In late 1943 30 GIAP again returned to the rear for replenishment, after which it was assigned to 273 IAD. The allocation of a Guards regiment to a regular division suggests that the regiment's performance may not have been up to the standards expected of the Guards. However, Mikhail Rents seems to have fulfilled his duties acceptably, even if he had scored only rarely, and since he had led his flight effectively, he was promoted to command the 3rd squadron.

During the summer of 1944 Rents at last began to achieve more personal successes whilst flying in support of Operation *Bagration* (the battle for Belorussia and Poland). For example, on 12 August, while providing air cover for the ground forces, his group shot down six Ju 87s from a force of 30, Rents personally claiming two of them. By the end of 1944 his squadron had earned the reputation of being the best not only in his regiment, but in the whole division, having flown 1183 sorties and scored 58 victories under his command. By year-end Rents was a major.

During the first four days of the Berlin operation his squadron flew 112 sorties and scored 15 victories. By the end of April Rents had flown 246 missions, and in 56 aerial combats he scored 18 individual (2 Bf 109s, 12 Fw 190s, 1 Ju 88 and 3 Ju 87s) and 5 shared victories. Nine of these victories were scored in April 1945 alone, including three Fw 190s shot down on the 17th, two more on the 18th and a further pair on the 20th. More action followed in early May, and Rents finished the war having flown a total of 261 sorties and 63 aerial combats, with 20 individual and 5 shared kills to his credit. He was awarded the HSU on 15 May 1946.

Mikhail Rents remained in the air force after the war, and for two years served as the Inspector for Flight Proficiency with 64 YAK – the head-quarters unit for Soviet fighter units fighting over Korea. And while he may have flown some combat missions in MiG-15s, there is no evidence that he did so very often, or ever claimed any victories.

The other leading pilot of 30 GIAP was Aleksandr Petrovich Filatov, who arrived at the front as a sergeant pilot in March 1943 and flew in Mikhail Rents' 3rd squadron. He scored his first victory on 9 May against a Fw 190, and then on 2 June downed a Bf 110 over Kursk. He was quiet, modest and a lover of literature, especially poetry. After his first victory, when he returned to his base, he remained seated in the cockpit recovering his self control, before getting out of the aeroplane and calmly announcing his success as if it hardly mattered. He seems to have been even more talented than his commander.

Within three months Filatov had scored eight individual and four shared victories, including three kills in one mission on 5 July – the first day of the Battle of Kursk. He was shot down on this mission, however, being forced to bail out. Fortunately for him, the wind carried his parachute back over Soviet lines, and the next morning he rejoined the regiment. Six days later Filatov was again downed by Fw 190s, but this time he landed on the German side of the lines. Knocked unconscious when he hit the ground, he was soon captured. However, on 15 August he escaped together with a Soviet tank crewman when their column was strafed. For over a month Filatov evaded recapture, before returning to his unit.

Of course this was a very serious matter, for even the briefest captivity was considered treason under Soviet military regulations. However, Filatov passed the SMERSh investigation, and 30 GIAP's CO, Col Khasan Ibatullin returned him to combat duty after considering his case.

During the summer of 1944 Filatov was promoted to senior lieutenant, and he became the deputy commander of Mikhail Rents' 3rd squadron.

The final months of 1944 and early 1945 proved a quiet time for 30 GIAP, as the Germans husbanded their dwindling resources and seldom challenged the Soviets. In March Filatov was appointed commander of the 1st squadron, and with the start of the final drive toward Berlin just weeks later, the Germans threw all their remaining resources into the last battle. Filatov scored a further eight victories in the final weeks of the war, including two kills on 19 April.

The following day, however, during an evening patrol, the ace was again shot down. With his P-39 in flames, Filatov had to make a belly landing in German-controlled territory. As he sprang from the cockpit and tried to dash for a nearby wood, he was shot in the leg by a burst of machine gun fire and captured for a second time. Taken to a German hospital, Filatov escaped at the first opportunity and returned to his regiment. He was again cleared of blame, and had the full support of his commanders. Filatov was even promoted to captain, but being captured twice was a guarantee that he would not get the HSU, or have a career in the air force postwar. He left the service in 1946. Filatov flew 175 missions, fought 35 combats and scored 21 individual and 4 shared kills.

As 1943 progressed the first P-39N/Qs began to arrive across the AlSib (Alaskan-Siberian) Trace in large numbers, and more regiments were thrown into action equipped with these later models. Two of the most outstanding from this period were 27 IAP, which converted in May 1943, and 9 GIAP, which received *Kobras* in August. The latter unit was known as 'the Regiment of Aces', and it was the one outfit in the Soviet Air Forces whose renown might match that of 16 GIAP, after whom it ranked third in order of accomplishments with 558 victories.

The regiment had begun the war as 69 IAP, equipped with the I-16, and it had distinguished itself in the defence of Odessa and the Southern Ukraine. Awarded its Guards number on 7 March 1942 (the same day as 16 GIAP), it had switched to LaGGs and Yak-1s during the course of the year. In October 1942 9 GIAP had been reorganised as an elite regiment manned by hand-picked aces, all of whom had been transferred in from other regiments within the 8th Air Army. Pilots were assigned to 9 GIAP 'on probation', and those who did not prove themselves by scoring victories in the first couple of weeks, or who otherwise failed to meet the commander's standards were sent down to some other regiment, where they generally proved themselves very superior – just not quite superior enough for the 9 GIAP.

In August 1943 this elite regiment was re-equipped with the P-39L, and other variants, although it subsequently flew the *Kobra* for just ten months. In July 1944 9 GIAP was withdrawn from the front to convert to the new Lavochkin La-7, and thus become one of the few units to actually replace its P-39s with another fighter type.

Although the identity of this pilot remains unclear, it is almost certainly Snr Lt Pavel Golovachyov of 9 GIAP. The red lightning bolt on the side of the fuselage was the unit's distinctive wartime marking, and it later appeared on the regiment's La-7s. Note the photo and the artwork of a woman overlapping the '4' – both highly unusual markings on Soviet aircraft, even in these chaste renditions. This photo was probably taken in late 1943, shortly after Golovachyov had received his first HSU. He ended the war as a captain with 31 individual and 1 shared victories, and received a second HSU on 29 June 1945 (*via Petrov*)

Perhaps the 'ace of aces' within 9 GIAP at this time was Sultan Amet-Khan, the twice HSU Tartar from the Crimea who ended the war with 30 individual and 19 shared victories. When Amet-Khan was transferred from 4 IAP to 9 GIAP, one of his former comrades said, 'The regiment without Amet-Khan is like a wedding without music'. He began the war flying the I-153, and later the Hurricane, with 4 IAP, and went almost a year before scoring his first victory. Finally, on 31 May 1942, Amet-Khan succeeded in bringing down a Ju 88 by *taran*.

He had been forced to resort to such desperate measures after making a bet with the regiment's Political Officer that he would score a victory before the end of the month – the prize was a silver cigarette case, which he wanted badly! After ramming the bomber Amet-Khan bailed out, and when he landed local villagers were so confused by his accent and non-Russian appearance that they took him prisoner and confined him together with his recent German victims, until the army arrived to sort things out! Within a month Amet-Khan had raised his score to seven kills.

Excitable and eager before the battle, on the ground he was known for his jokes and merriment. Each night on the way back to his quarters, it was Amet-Khan's habit to pull out his pistol and fire a single shot into the air, announcing his salute 'For the living' – on the evening in October 1942 when told of his selection to join 9 GIAP he fired off four shots! His new unit welcomed him as a captain, and CO of the 3rd squadron.

By the time 9 GIAP converted to the Airacobra in August 1943, Amet-Khan had already scored 19 individual and 11 shared victories, and he would soon receive his first HSU (on the 24th of that month). He quickly put the P-39 to work, downing two bombers over Kalinovka on 20 August. The following day his formation intercepted a dozen Ju 88s, and he duly shot one down, and he then tangled with a second formation of 15 He 111s and destroyed one of these as well.

During March 1944 Amet-Khan's squadron established a secret base behind German lines in order to disrupt Ju 52/3ms flying supplies to the Crimea – the Luftwaffe mistakenly believed that their vulnerable transports were operating beyond the range of Soviet fighters. It was during the campaign to liberate the Crimea that Amet-Khan had the pleasure of downing a Fw 190 which crashed near his home town of Alupka.

With the final victory in the Crimea, Amet-Khan and his family invited the entire 9 GIAP to his home for a three-day celebration. But victory soon turned sour for Stalin decided that the Crimea Tartars were collectively guilty of treason and collaboration with the Germans, and ordered the entire people deported to camps in Central Asia, where about a third perished within six months. Only a particularly courageous intervention by Gen Khryukin, commander of the 8th Air Army, gained an exemption for Amet-Khan's family, but not soon enough to save the ace's brother.

In July 1944 9 GIAP was sent to the rear to convert to the La-7, with which they finished the war. It is uncertain, but likely, that Amet-Khan scored six individual and eight shared victories while flying the P-39. He received his second HSU in June 1945.

Another 9 GIAP P-39 ace was Aleksei Alelyukhin, who started the war serving with 69 IAP, and was deputy commander of the 'regiment of aces' by May 1945. He originated the regiment custom of painting the spinners of the 1st squadron's fighters red, and this marking was soon adopted by the other units within 9 GIAP, which selected their own colours. In January 1943 he became the 1st squadron's CO. By the time he received his first HSU on 24 August 1943, Alelyukhin had scored 11 individual and 6 shared kills flying the I-16 and Yak-1, and by November 1943, when he received his second HSU, he had increased his individual score to 26 kills (the bulk of these were claimed with the P-39).

On 5 May 1944 Alelyukhin downed a Fw 190 over the Crimea, but his own P-39 was damaged and he was forced to bail out. He drifted down between German and Soviet positions that were already engaged in combat, and the fight intensified as both sides attempted to retrieve the pilot. It was Alelyukhin's good fortune that his Red Army comrades prevailed.

In July, when the regiment was withdrawn to convert to the La-7, Alelyukhin was appointed deputy commander. In October 9 GIAP returned to the front in East Prussia, and by war's end Aleksei Alelyukhin had completed 601 sorties and scored 40 individual and 17 shared kills (26 and 11 in the P-39). Just as important was the fact that he acted as a mentor for inexperienced pilots, and he helped many aces gain their first victories.

Another leading ace assigned to 9 GIAP was Vladimir Lavrinenkov. A frustrated instructor upon the outbreak of war, when he finally reached a combat unit he found it equipped with antiquated I-15s until the spring of 1942, when the first Yak-1s finally arrived. Lavrinenkov was issued with 'White 17', which he warmly welcomed for his birthday was on 17 May (1919). Indeed, for the rest of the war, his aircraft was always '17'.

At last equipped with a credible fighter, Lavrinenkov began to achieve success, and in October 1942 he was among the pilots selected for 9 GIAP. On one occasion, in June 1943, the ace fought so tenaciously that he was ordered to report to Gen Khryukin, commander of the 8th Air Army. The general had seen him in action from the ground, and he heartily congratulated Lavrinenkov and presented him to Front Commander Gen Tolbukhin, who in turn awarded him a gold watch.

By the time the unit re-equipped with P-39s in August 1943, Lavrinenkov had become a senior lieutenant, a deputy squadron commander and HSU recipient (awarded on 1 May 1943). He had scored 22 individual and 11 shared victories, and within days of returning to the front Lavrinenkov had downed three more aircraft.

Then on 24 August he made the serious mistake of going in combat without 'White 17'. His regiment commander had ordered him to knock down a Fw 189 *Rama* which was bothering the troops, and since Lavrinenkov's '17' was grounded for maintenance, his CO told him to borrow his own 'White 01'. The *Rama* proved particularly evasive, and Lavrinenkov used all his ammunition.

Meanwhile Air Army Commander Gen Khryukin, who had been observing the action from his command post called on the radio 'Seventeen – I don't recognise you!' Lavrinenkov responded, 'I – Sokol Seventeen. Now you'll see!' Making a close pass, he struck the *Rama's* tail with his wingtip and was forced to bail out. Losing the commander's aircraft may have been poor form, but worse was to come, for the wind blew Lavrinenkov's parachute westward. When he finally landed the ace was captured by German troops before he could even get out of the parachute harness! Lavrinenkov eventually managed to escape from a PoW train heading for Germany, and headed eastward until he encountered a

Another unidentified junior lieutenant serving with a P-39-equipped Guards regiment in 1944. The name penned on the original photograph is only partially clear, and does not identify any of the known aces or commanders (*Russian Aviation Research Trust*)

partisan group. Lavrinenkov remained with the partisans fighting behind enemy lines until advancing Soviet tanks made contact with them.

Reunited with Soviet regular forces, Lavrinenkov was flown back to headquarters, where Gens Khryukin and Tolbukhin debriefed him. The ace was eager to return to his unit, but Gen Tolbukhin told him that he could not go back without shoulder boards, and then instructed an adjutant to go and get him a captain's boards.

A few days later he arrived back at 9 GIAP, and was given a hero's welcome. However, the unavoidable unpleasantness with SMERSh kept Lavrinenkov out of the air for a bit longer, and it was not until 24 October that he returned to the air, and promptly shot down a German bomber. During the spring of 1944 he was one of the pilots who flew from the secret base behind enemy lines, shooting down his 11th, and last, P-39 victory on 5 May from this site when he claimed a Fw 190 over Sevastopol. By the time Lavrinenkov next saw combat he had converted to the La-7, which he used to bring his tally of kills to 36 by war's end.

Yet another regiment to re-equip with the P-39 in 1943 was 27 IAP, which had spent the first year of the war assigned to the Moscow PVO district. In the summer of 1942 it was sent to the Stalingrad Front, and in the spring of 1943 the unit converted to the P-39 and was assigned to 205 IAD – on 8 October 1943 the regiment was redesignated 129 GIAP. Its commander from April 1943 was one of the greatest, but least known, Soviet aces, Vladimir Bobrov. He flew 451 sorties and scored a total of 30 individual and 20 shared victories, plus two Me 262s destroyed on the ground. Bobrov had also fought in the Spanish Civil War, flying 126 sorties and claiming 13 individual and 4 shared victories.

He had claimed his first kill of World War 2 on the first day of Operation *Barbarossa*, and his last on the final day of the conflict, and of the novice fighter pilots Bobrov trained between June 1941 and May 1945, 31 of them won the HSU. For some reason he never personally received the HSU, or any of the other official awards that fell copiously to other, lesser Soviet aces. Whatever the nature of his problem, whether it was 'political' or a blunt and outspoken manner, he seems to have made enemies of men in power – and with long memories. Whatever Bobrov's offence was, it seems not to have happened until later in the war, because after early combat in 1941-42, followed by a break for staff training, the veteran ace was appointed commander of 27 IAP on 4 April 1943.

The regiment distinguished itself at Kursk and the subsequent Belgorod-Kharkov offensive, scoring 55 victories. In a typical mission for this period, on 6 July Bobrov led 10 P-39s to intercept a group of 27 Ju 87s and 12 Bf 109s. In the ensuing fight, the Soviet pilots successfully repelled the raiders, and each claimed a kill apiece while suffering no losses themselves. At the beginning of 1944, for no discernible reason, Bobrov was removed from command of his regiment.

Surviving members of 27 IAP remember him as a good commander, as well as an excellent pilot and affable character. It seems almost certain that high-ranking military officials held an animus against him, which seems to have followed his career. As was typical in the Soviet Union during this period, a man removed from a command position became 'infectious', and nobody would approach him or offer him a new military assignment. Only Pokryshkin, who was acquainted with Bobrov only via aerial radio transmissions and reputation, had the strength of character and personal authority to welcome him into his division. He made him CO of 104 GIAP in May, and Bobrov demonstrated that the trust was well placed.

His greatest day came during September when he and his wingman attacked a formation of He 111s, shooting down three bombers apiece. Still flying a P-39 at war's end, Bobrov's final victory came on 9 May 1945 over Czechoslovakia. Nominated for the HSU during the final months of the conflict, the ace was denied the award both by Chief Marshal Novikov, and later by Chief Marshal Vershinin. Whatever Vladimir Bobrov's offence, it left a long memory. In 1971 he died in obscurity, but on 20 March 1991 his exploits were belatedly recognised by Boris Yeltsin when the P-39 ace became one of the last people to receive the HSU.

Another ace who had trouble with his superior officers was Fyodor Arkhipenko. Assigned to 17 IAP in June 1941, Arkhipenko's unit was based at the badly-damaged airfield at Rostov-on-Don in the opening days of the campaign, and it was whilst here that he first got into trouble. He and several other pilots who had been assigned to the duty flight were seemingly forgotten by the combat-weary unit, and after sitting for three full days in the cockpits of their aircraft without relief, they fell asleep.

Their plight significantly worsened when they were discovered by the commander of the Military District, who ordered them shot without waiting to find out the circumstances. It was whilst facing a firing squad that Arkhipenko took the lead in saving the group when he suggested that it would be just as effective to send them to the front. With the support of the regiment commander, the pilots were spared.

Arkhipenko threw himself into defeating the Germans, and during a ground attack mission in October he attempted to save one of his comrades who had been shot down behind enemy lines. Unfortunately,

The four-bladed Aeroproducts propeller fitted to a P-39Q-25 partially frames a line-up of factory-fresh three-bladed Q-30s awaiting collection from Bell's Buffalo, New York, plant in 1944. Some 5578 P-39s were supplied to the USSR between December 1941 and February 1945 (*IWM*)

Aleksandr Pokryshkin (centre, wearing the flying helmet) is congratulated by his squadronmates after yet another successful sortie. His medals and the kill markings on his P-39 behind him suggest that this photo was taken some time in 1944 (*via D Maksimov*)

Maverick P-39 ace Grigorii Rechkalov smiles for the camera alongside his 'star-struck' P-39. Note that all the victory stars on his fighter are outlined in white, unlike those painted on his *Kobra* on page 77 (*Russian Aviation Research Trust*)

he damaged the landing gear of his fighter during the landing and now found himself stranded in German territory as well. Quickly swapping their flying suits for civilian clothes, they managed to travel eastwards through enemy territory and back to their own side after ten days. Following an interrogation by SMERSh, both pilots were allowed to rejoin their unit.

Arkhipenko was scoring victories during this period, but due to personal friction that existed between him and the regiment commander, he was frequently denied credit. During the Battle of Kursk, for example, he shot down 12 aircraft but was credited with only the two that he had destroyed over his own airfield, in full view of the entire regiment – the other ten kills were credited only as group victories. He was also denied medals which were only awarded to him after the war.

During the Kursk campaign, Arkhipenko was severely wounded in the leg and arm – doctors even considered amputating the latter limb. However, within two weeks he had returned to the front, but was now assigned as a squadron commander to P-39-equipped 508 IAP. Arkhipenko again failed to impress his regimental CO, and he was soon swapped for another 'difficult' ace, Pavel Chepinoga. Arkhipenko was in turn sent to 27 IAP as a senior lieutenant, where he was given command of the 1st squadron.

The ace fared much better with his new unit, forging a friendship with fellow ace Nikolai Gulaev. Arkhipenko may also have appreciated the fact that his new regiment commander was Vladimir Bobrov, who, as previously recounted in this volume, also had difficulty with military authorities. As a combat leader, Arkhipenko proved a success, and his squadron suffered minimal losses. Its best day came on 23 March 1944 when the ace led a flight of four P-39s in an interception against a *gruppe* of Stukas, shooting down eight of the Ju 87s before landing in a field near the banks of the Dnestr because they were low on fuel. During the Jassy-Kishinev operation Arkhipenko was personally successful, scoring 11 victories. By the end of the war he had attained the rank of major, and was the regiment's deputy commander.

Fyodor Arkhipenko completed 467 sorties and officially scored 30 individual and 14 shared kills. Never shot down, he was awarded the HSU on 27 June 1945.

Arkhipenko's friend Nikolai Gulaev was another outstanding Airacobra ace. At the beginning of the war he was assigned to an air defence regiment situated away

from the front, and he saw no action until April 1942. On one occasion he took off without orders during a night raid and by moonlight downed a He 111. In February 1943 Gulaev completed a course for flight commanders and was sent to 27 IAP, where he established his reputation.

By June 1943 he was a senior lieutenant and a deputy squadron commander, having scored 16 individual and 2 shared kills in 95 missions. One of these kills was by *taran* on 14 May 1943. Gulaev intercepted a formation of Stukas and shot down the formation leader. Attacking a second bomber, he managed to silence the rear gunner but then ran out of ammunition, so he closed in and rammed the Ju 87 with his wing. His own aircraft was damaged enough that the ace then bailed out.

He particularly distinguished himself in the Battle of Kursk, and on the opening day of this pivotal clash (5 July) Gulaev flew six sorties and shot down four aircraft. On the 6th he destroyed a Fw 190, on the 7th he claimed a Ju 87 as an individual victory and a Fw 189 and Hs 126 as group kills, on the 8th he shot down a Bf 109 and on the 9th he destroyed two bombers over Belgorod, one of them by *taran*. Three days later Gulaev was appointed commander of the 2nd squadron.

The regiment then withdrew in order to re-equip with new P-39s, before returning to the front in August. On the 9th Gulaev downed a Ju 87, followed by a Ju 88 two days later and a pair of Bf 109s on the 12th. This scoring run brought him the HSU on 28 September. In January and February 1944 he flew in support of the battle for Kirovograd, and then the Korsun-Shevchenkovskii operation. In March Gulaev enjoyed a brief leave home, but he returned in April and claimed ten kills in two weeks.

His first victories during this period came on the 18th when he downed two Ju 87s and a Bf 109 while providing aerial cover for ground forces in the Shera region. Exactly one week later Gulaev shot down four Fw 190s in a single combat over Dubossary, his wingman claiming two kills during the same mission. Four other members of his formation also destroyed another five Fw 190s, all for no losses.

On 30 May Gulaev again downed four aircraft when he destroyed a Hs 126, a Ju 87 and two Bf 109s. However, in his last sortie of the day he was wounded in the leg, and the ace only just made it back to base – the remaining five members of his formation were all shot down, with one being killed and one posted missing. A brief stay in hospital ensued, but he soon returned to his regiment, and on 1 July he was awarded his second HSU for having scored a further 42 individual and 3 shared victories.

By August 1944 Gulaev had been promoted to major, and he downed Fw 190s on the 10th, 11th and 12th of that month. Forty-eight hours later he fought his last aerial battle. While flying with a novice on his wing, he was bounced by German fighters and badly shot up. Although wounded yet again, Gulaev turned into his opponents and shot down two of them before breaking off and escaping. Crash-landing back at his airfield, the ace

Four well known P-39 aces pose together for the camera in front of Grigorii Rechkalov's *Kobra* in mid-1944. They are, from left to right, Capt Aleksandr Klubov, Maj Grigorii Rechkalov, Lt Andrei Trud and Maj Boris Glinka. The presence of the latter pilot wearing his major's shoulder boards establish that this photograph must have been taken between early June, when he was promoted and then replaced Rechkalov as 16 GIAP commander, and 15 July, when he was seriously injured bailing out of his P-39. The solitary Gold Star of the HSU on Rechkalov's uniform further limits the time period to before 1 July. One may guess that this shot was taken shortly after the change of command, with the primary purpose of the gathering being to attest to formal regiment harmony. None of the pilots appears particularly jolly, however! (*via Petrov*)

This was the famous P-39N-0 (42-9033) flown firstly by Ivan Babak and then by Grigorii Dol'nikov – both high-scoring *Kobra* aces with 100 GIAP. This photograph, and the one at the bottom of this page, were obviously taken after Babak's disappearance in combat on 22 April 1945, and may commemorate either the fall of Berlin or the German surrender. The inscription on the left side of the fighter read *From the Schoolchildren of Mariupol*, although the construction of this P-39 had in fact been funded by the US taxpayer! (*via Petrov*)

The accompanying right side view of Babak/Dol'nikov's P-39N-0. The latter ace had the inscription *For Petya Guschyok* applied to the right side of the fighter after he had inherited it from Babak (*via Petrov*)

was rushed to hospital, although on this occasion he did not recover in time to return to operations before the hostilities had ended. These final kills raised his total to 57 individual and 3 shared victories, including 4 by *taran*.

On 2 May 1944 9 GIAD, now led by Col Pokryshkin, returned to the front and joined in the action in the Jassy-Kishinev campaign, which destroyed Germany's southern front and knocked Romania out of the war. Following this comprehensive victory, 9 GIAP transferred north for the Lvov-Sandomir operation, and finally the invasion of Germany.

Pokryshkin now had the administrative and command responsibilities of a division commander, although he still found time for combat. On 18 July he scored two kills, followed by a high altitude German recce aircraft days later. The following month Pokryshkin became the first member of the armed forces to receive a third HSU for completing 550 missions by May 1944, and scoring 53 individual and 6 shared kills in 137 combats, while at the same time showing outstanding leadership.

Although Pokryshkin was coping admirably with his new position, his successor at 16 GIAP, Grigorii Rechkalov, was not doing so well. Shortly after his appointment one of his pilots was killed due to the carelessness of a mechanic, and then on 31 May he was involved in a disastrous battle over Jassy. Messerschmitts succeeded in getting between the strike group led by Rechkalov and the covering group led by Klubov, and five P-39s were swiftly downed. 16 GIAP's CO was immediately stripped of his command by Pokryshkin 'for losing control, indecisiveness and lack of initiative', and he was replaced by 100 GIAP's Boris Glinka.

Despite his demotion Rechkalov kept flying, and by June he had completed 415 missions and engaged in 112 combats. His score stood at 48 individual and 6 shared kills, and he won his second HSU on 1 July.

Two weeks later, on 15 July, Boris Glinka was wounded in action when he bailed out of his badly damaged P-39 and struck its tailplane. Breaking his collar bone and both legs, he was unable to return to combat before war's end, so Rechkalov was made CO of 16 GIAP once again. Rechkalov and Pokryshkin continued to clash, however, the latter believing in teamwork and military discipline, which were both qualities that Rechkalov sorely lacked. Indeed, the great ace had always been notorious for his indiscipline in flight, breaking formation to chase individual victories, and personal glory. Rechkalov was again relieved of command in February 1945 and assigned to division headquarters, where he continued to fly, but had no command responsibilities. By VE-Day Grigorii

Rechkalov had flown 450 sorties and engaged in 122 combats, claiming 56 individual and 6 shared victories.

In February 1945 9 GIAD crossed into Germany, the division penetrating so far that it could not find a suitable airfield. Pokryshkin solved the problem by improvising – he landed on a section of German autobahn and decided that it would make a good runway. The division followed him down and quickly began operating from the highways, taking special care to camouflage and conceal its aircraft from prying German reconnaissance aircraft. This move caused consternation amongst the enemy, who struggled to ascertain where the P-39s were flying from.

Numerous low-level flights and ground reconnaissance patrols were conducted in order to locate Pokryshkin's base, and eventually the autobahn 'airstrip' was discovered. The Luftwaffe immediately launched a series of raids on the highways, but they still had trouble finding the camouflaged targets. Several aircraft were damaged, however, and one of 16 GIAP's squadron commanders, Capt Tsvetkov was killed on the ground.

After Rechkalov was appointed Inspector for Flight Training of 9 GIAD, Ivan Babak was given command of 16 GIAP, although his period in charge only lasted to 22 April, when he was shot down by flak and captured. Although a PoW for just two weeks, Babak's promising career was permanently ruined – to make matters worse, he was shot down on Lenin's birthday! This misfortune cost him a second HSU, and had it not been for Pokryshkin's direct support, it could have cost him far more. By the time of his capture Babak had flown 330 missions and scored a total of 33 individual and 4 group victories.

Another curious development in those last days of war was the interception of a strange contraption by 15-kill ace Capt Mikhail Petrov of 100 GIAP. He had been vectored onto a German formation, and once in visual sight of his target he reported via radio that he'd seen a 'two-storey wonder' – a Junkers bomber with a Messerschmitt attached on top via a frame, with all three engines running. The division intelligence officer reported this to Pokryshkin, who gave the order to shoot it down, but to be very careful to shoot only at the fighter. Petrov did so, and when the *Mistel* crashed there was a tremendous explosion.

Pokryshkin continued flying until VE-Day, by which time he had completed 650 sorties and engaged in 156 combats. He was officially credited with 59 individual and 6 group victories, although he maintained that he actually scored 72 individual kills, including those which could not be confirmed because they crashed too far behind enemy lines. In addition to his own victories, 30 pilots under his command were made HSUs, with several receiving the award twice! Although ranking Soviet ace Ivan Kozhedub's total of 62 individual kills exceeds Pokryshkin's 59, the additional shared victories, and his crucial role in training other aces, marks him out as 'both the Boelcke and the Richthofen of the Soviet Air Force'.

The Soviet Air Force's ranking aces are seen together in the Kremlin in late August 1945. Aleksandr Pokryshkin (left) and Ivan Kozhedub had just been presented with their third Gold Stars (visible above their respective campaign ribbons), the latter ace's award being dated 18 August 1945 and Pokryshkin's 19 August 1945 (*via Petrov*)

CAMOUFLAGE AND MARKINGS

Throughout the war, the Soviet Union left its lend-lease aircraft in their original delivery schemes (except for some temporary winter finishes), changing only the national markings. This meant that the Airacobra Is shipped from Britain arrived in standard RAF Fighter Command camouflage of Dark Green and Dark Sea Grey upper surfaces, and Medium Sea Grey undersides – spinners were typically Sky Type S. And while some of the early Airacobra Is retained the Sky Type S fuselage band, most did not. However, all kept their original British serial numbers in the AH, AP, BX and BW series.

The British national markings were simply painted over upon the fighters' arrival in the Soviet Union, the roundels on the upper surfaces with 'Russian' Green A-24m (generally about FSN 34102, but ranging from 34095 to 34151, depending on the field-mixed batch) and those on the undersides with Light Blue A-28m (FSN 25190) – the latter paint only partially obscured the RAF roundels. Soviet red stars were in turn painted on over these areas, and in late 1941 and early 1942, these had either no border or occasionally a narrow black outline.

During the course of late 1942 the traditional narrow white outlined star was introduced, and eventually it became standard in 1943. Occasionally, this white border was replaced by yellow, although examples of this are rare. In Soviet practice the aircraft's two digit 'bort' number could be placed either on the fuselage side, or the tail, or occasionally even the nose of the aircraft. The decision on placement seems to have been left up to the regiment, with 19 GIAP, for example, applying its numbers in large white 'Slavic Style' figures on the vertical tail surfaces of its *Kobras*. Placement of numbers by other regiments flying the Airacobra I has not been determined, although it appears that aircraft assigned to depot units may not have used numbers at all.

American P-39s all arrived in standard Dark Olive Drab uppersurfaces and Neutral Gray undersides. In addition to the standard US insignia in four places (fuselage and upper left and lower right wing surfaces), each aircraft also wore a standard six-digit yellow serial number across the tail surfaces. On P-39Ds, and many later examples, the Soviets did not bother overpainting the American insignia. Instead, they simply applied the red star directly over the white one on the blue roundel, although this was often slightly larger in size, and extended beyond the disc.

As with the Airacobra I, these stars initially had either no border, or just a thin black outline, and later a white border. On the wing surfaces, this produced an asymmetric effect, with a star on a dark blue circle on one side, and a plain star on the other. The yellow serial number was usually left intact too, and the bort number – typically white – was often located on the fuselage aft of the national insignia. Occasionally, the serial number, along with the American national insignias, were overpainted with Russian green. Since this overpainting was done under unit conditions, modellers are urged not be excessively precise.

As wartime production increased, and batches of aircraft – particularly P-39s – were earmarked for the Russians while still on the production lines, a number of markings developments occurred. Some aircraft were finished by the Bell factory with Soviet insignia already applied, thus presenting the traditional Russian Star painted directly on Olive Drab, with no blue circle, or Russian Green-overpainted background.

From 11 September 1943 the Soviet star also experienced change, officially gaining the narrow (10 mm) red outline around the white border (50 mm). From this date onwards we can find examples of the red star on a blue disk, although it now features the white border and red outline.

Some time during the course of 1944 aircraft began to receive a new Russian 'transit' insignia consisting of the red star on the background of a white circle, generally appearing in all six positions. Photos of this presentation are relatively rare, and these insignias may have been overpainted upon arrival in the Soviet Union. However, some *Kobras* did go to the front with their white circles intact, as evidenced by the famous photograph of a late model P-39 from Pokryshkin's division taking off from a German autobahn in 1945. All of these variations existed simultaneously, and examples might be found side-by-side in a single regiment.

A further unusual variation of Soviet national markings has recently been confirmed – some P-39s substituted silver (or aluminium) paint for white both for their bort numbers and for the borders of their red stars. A fighter thought to be from 191 IAP that was salvaged from a Finnish forest, and restored at the Finnish Air Force Museum, has the doubly unusual combination of red stars with silver border and red outline, on a white circle. Other aircraft from 191 IAP featured the silver borders without the white 'transit circle'. This regiment also painted the rudders of its P-39Ns silver, and placed their silver bort numbers on the nose of the aeroplane, just ahead of the cockpit.

The one local variation in Airacobra painting was temporary winter white camouflage, and this seems to have been rarely applied. The Russian temporary white paint was notorious both for its poor quality and for its negative effect on the performance of aircraft, and so was used only when absolutely necessary. It would not have been inflicted on aircraft used by depot training units, and was not needed come May 1942, when 19 GIAP flew the first Airacobra I sorties.

By the winter of 1943-44, the Soviets had achieved sufficient mastery of the air that they no longer felt they needed to bother with the difficult winter camouflage for most of their aircraft. This leaves only the winter of 1942-43, when winter camouflage could very well have been applied to P-39s by regiments based in the north on the Leningrad and Karelian Fronts. Here, too, there seem to have been exceptions, with at least one regiment winter-camouflaging its P-39s not with the despised artificial white, but with metallic paint! On both the white and metallic finishes, bort numbers were typically presented in red.

One error perpetuated in post-war publications discussing the operations of ex-RAF Airacobra Is in Russia is that they have often been represented in Dark Green and Dark Earth camouflage. However, all

Kobras which arrived from Britain were painted in the newer Dark Green-Dark Ocean Grey scheme. Any examples so camouflaged that served in the USSR could only have come from P-400 stocks supplied directly from the United States.

The least understood aspect of Soviet P-39 markings is the application of formation and individual markings, and donation inscriptions. Markings intended to distinguish units began to see some use in late 1943, and grew in popularity in 1944. For example, by the autumn of 1943 the P-39s of Pokryshkin's 16 GIAP had had their vertical fin tips painted red, while 100 GIAP (in the same division) seems to have used an identical marking, but in white. Finally, aircraft with a red fin tip bordered in white may have also been 16 GIAP machines, or possibly 9 GIAD Division command *zveno*.

P-39s of 5 GIAD's 68 GIAP sported a medium blue band, with white borders, around the rear of the fuselage and the spinner in the same colour – white bort numbers were painted on the nose. 72 GIAP of 5 GIAD

This P-39Q-15 belonged to either 68 or 72 GIAP, depending on whether the fuselage band and spinner were medium blue or red, respectively. Both Guards regiments served with 5 GIAD

This P-39N was one of six assigned to 21 GIAP in 1943 that had supposedly been paid for by the citizens of Krasnoyarsk – the slogan on its side reads *Krasnoyarskii Komsomolets*. The fighter is seen in Siberia prior to the regiment returning to the front in the Ukraine (*via Petrov*)

substituted red for the fuselage band and spinner colours. No photographs exist showing that either 28 or 67 GIAPs used similar bands in other colours, although it would not be surprising if such evidence surfaces in the future. However, a yellow fuselage band would be most unlikely, for it could have easily caused confusion with the Luftwaffe's standard theatre marking. Other units featured either narrow or wide diagonal bands on the vertical tail and rudder, which might have been either established unit or temporary tactical markings. Another known example of a unit marking saw Northern Fleet's 255 IAP paint the tail fin tips of its P-39s white in a similar style to that adopted by 100 GIAP.

While the spinners fitted to the original Airacobra Is came painted in Sky Type S, American P-39s arrived with camouflaged spinners. In turn, the Soviets would often overpaint these to indicate a regiment within a division, and sometimes the squadron within the regiment – on other occasions spinners were painted metallic, and then polished. In 9 GIAP spinner colours denoted different units, with Alelyukhin's 1st squadron in red, Kovachevich's 2nd in blue and Amet-Khan's 3rd in yellow.

Red was a favourite colour for Guards regiments, and when flying the Yak-1 55 GIAP had a tradition of reserving red spinners for donation aircraft. It is unknown, but highly probable, that this tradition was continued after the unit transitioned to the P-39.

And yes, there were lend-lease P-39s that bore inscriptions indicating that they had been 'bought' for the Soviet Air Force with the voluntary contributions of Soviet citizens, however offensive that might be to the American taxpayers who had originally bought and contributed those P-39s. Examples included ten P-39s 'bought' for 21 GIAP in 1943, four of which were inscribed *Krasnoyarskii Komsomolets*, four *Krasnoyarskii Rabochii* and two *Krasnoyarskii Kolkhoznik* (*Krasnoyarsk Komsomol* member, worker and collective farmer, respectively). On occasion, aircraft with dedication names did not display bort numbers.

Maj Vyacheslav Sirotin flew this stunningly marked P-39 whilst serving with 17 IAP in the Baltic region and northern Poland during late 1944. A veteran of over 330 combat missions, Sirotin ended the war with 26 victories, all of which were scored in the P-39. Following the defeat of Germany, 17 IAP quickly converted onto the P-63 Kingcobra and was transferred east to the 12th Air Army, where Sirotin participated in the brief war against Japan. During this short conflict, his wingman scored the only aerial victory recorded by the P-63 (*via Petrov*)

Capt Aleksei Zakalyuk of 104 GIAP smiles for the camera from the cockpit of his personalised P-39 in Poland in September 1944. The 16-kill ace flew 594 missions and fought 90 engagements with the enemy during World War 2 (*via Petrov*)

Finally, there were individual markings. Whether to permit, forbid, or encourage individual markings and slogans was entirely the regiment or division commander's prerogative. K D Denisov, commander of 11 GIAP-ChF, made it clear in his memoir that he had no tolerance for such individualism. However, individual insignia were so frequent in Pokryshkin's 16 GIAP and 9 GIAD, that they seem to have been encouraged. Known markings include Zakalyuk's 'tiger', Grafin's 'ace of spades', Bobrov's 'bogey man' and, most famous of all, the extravagantly marked aircraft flown by Ivan Babak and inherited by Grigorii Dol'nikov (see the colour profiles for examples of these aircraft).

The final area to be examined covers victory markings. The Soviet practice was to paint small stars for each kill, and these were applied in different locations on the aircraft according to the taste of the pilot or unit tradition. Underneath the cockpit, above the exhausts, on the cockpit door or on the nose were the most common locations on the P-39. Some pilots used stars of more than one colour (generally red and white or red and yellow stars), and these distinguished individual from shared victories, or fighters from bombers, depending on the ace's prerogative.

The pilot in this photo has been identified as Guards Lt F I Shikunov, about whom little is known. The Order of Nevskii painted on the cockpit door, together with the location of the aircraft number on the nose suggest that this aircraft served with 69 IAP/9 GIAP. Shikunov is known to have flown with this unit, and he reputedly claimed as many as 25 kills in 1944-45 (*via Petrov*)

A PENDICES

APPENDIX I

USAAF aces who scored at least one kill in the P-39/P-400

Name	P-39 Score	Total Score
Lt William F Fiedler Jr	5	5
Capt Francis E Dubisher	4	5
Lt Thomas J Lynch	3	20
Lt Donald C McGee	3*	6
Capt John W Mitchell	3	11
Col Boyd D Wagner	3	8
Lt George S Welch	3	16
Maj Paul S Bechtel	2	5
Lt Hugh D Dow	2**	2
Lt Alvaro J Hunter	2	5
Lt William F McDonough	2	5
Lt Daniel T Roberts	2	14
Lt Clifton H Troxell	2	5
Lt Robert R Yaeger	2	5
Lt Frank Adkins	1	5
Lt Zed D Fountain	1***	4.5 unconfirmed
Lt Grover D Gholson	1	5
Lt Verl E Jett	1	7
Lt Curran L Jones	1	5
Lt Joseph T McKeon	1	6
Lt William H Strand	1	7
Lt Richard C Suehr	1	5
Lt Charles P Sullivan	1	5

* claims as many as 5 kills in P-39
** perhaps ranking P-39 pilot in MTO
*** as many as 5.5 victories in unit records

APPENDIX II

P-39 Airacobras provided under Lend-Lease to the USSR

Airacobra I	158 of 212 sent
P-39D	108
P-39K	40
P-39L	137
P-39M	157
P-39N	1113
P-39Q	3291

APPENDIX III

Identified P-39 Airacobra Units*

6 GIAK	
9 GIAD	16, 100 and 104 GIAP (plus 159 GIAP with La-7 from 11/44)
22 GIAD	129, 212 and 213 GIAP
23 GIAD	21 and 69 GIAP
1 GIAD	54 and 55 GIAP (plus 53 and 56 GIAP with Yak-9)
5 GIAD	28, 67, 68 and 72 GIAP
1 GSAD	19 and 20 GIAP (plus 17 GShAP with Il-2m and 114 GBAP with Pe-2)
141 IAD-PVO	631 and 908 IAP
190 IAD	17 and 821 IAP
273 IAD	30 GIAP and 352 IAP
329 IAD	57 and 101 GIAP and 66 IAP
2 GIAK-PVO	102 and 103 GIAP and 403 IAP (plus 11 GIAP with La-5 and 26 and 27 GIAP both with Spitfire IX and Yak-9)

9 GIAP (303 IAD)
9 IAP (uncertain, possibly 304 IAD)
28 IAP (318 IAD-PVO)
185 IAP (disbanded 8/42)
191 IAP (275 IAD)
196 IAP (324 IAD)
246 IAP (215 IAD)
266 IAP (10 IAK-PVO)
295 IAP (uncertain)
416 IAP (possibly disbanded)
484 IAP (323 IAD)
494 IAP (303 IAD)
738 IAP (129 IAD-PVO)

* this list includes regiments which achieved Guards status only under their Guards designation

Naval Units

6 IAD-SF
2 GIAP-SF, 27 and 78 IAP-SF
11 GIAP-ChF (2 GMTAD)
20 IAP-SF (14 SAD-SF)
31 IAP-TOF (16 SAD)
43 IAP-ChF (13 PBAD)
255 IAP-SF (1 GMTAD-SF)

APPENDIX IV

Soviet P-39 Aces

Name	Rank	Award	Unit	Victories (Individual/shared)	sorties/combats	KIA
Adonkin, Vasilii Semyonovich	Maj	HSU	78 IAP-SF	16 and 6 (some in P-39)	365/42	17/3/44
Akinshin, S V	Jr Lt		129 GIAP	7	70/12	30/5/44
Alelyukhin, Aleksei Vasiliévich	Capt	2 x HSU	9 GIAP	40 and 17 (26/11 in P-39?)	601/258	
Amet-Khan, Sultan	Maj	2 x HSU	9 GIAP	30 and 19 (maybe 6/8 in P-39)	603/150	

Name	Rank	Award	Unit	Victories (Individual/shared)	sorties/combats	KIA
Arkhipenko, Fyodor Fyodorovich	Col	HSU	129 GIAP	30 and 14 (26/4 in P-39)	467/102	
Askirenko, Ivan	unknown		438 IAP	5 (4 in P-39, including 1 *taran*)		PoW ?/4/44
Avdeev, Aleksandr Fyodorovich	Sr Lt	HSU	153 IAP	11	189/?	2/10/43
Babaev, Aleksandr Ivanovich	Capt	HSU	196 IAP	9 and 1	260/48	
Babak, Ivan Il'ich	Capt	HSU	100 GIAP	33 and 4 (1 in Yak-1)	330/103	PoW 22/4/45
Baikov, Georgii Ivanovich	Sr Lt	HSU	9 GIAP	15 and 5 (some in Yak-1 and La-7)	244/50	
Balyuk, Ivan Fyodorovich	Maj	HSU	54 GIAP	25 and 5 (8 /2 in P-39)	500/135+	
Batyaev, Vasilii Sergeevich	Capt	HSU	54 GIAP	19 and 7 (some in I-16, LaGG and Yak)	639/234	
Bekashonok, Mikhail Vasil'ievich	Capt	HSU	129 GIAP	18 and 4	170/50	
Bendeliani, Chichiko Kaisarovich	Maj	HSU	54 GIAP	12 and 20 (5 /8 in P-39)	400/90	20/7/44
Berestnev, Pavel Maksimovich	Sr Lt	HSU	100 GIAP	12 and 12 (some in Yak)	131+/32+	
Berkutov, Aleksandr Maksimovich	Maj	HSU	101 GIAP	15	332+/68+	
Beryozkin, Vyacheslav A	Jr Lt		16 GIAP	12 (1 *taran*)		
Bilyukin, Aleksandr Dmitrievich	Capt	HSU	196 IAP	23 and 1 (some in I-16, P-40)	430/35	
Bobrov, Vladimir Ivanovich	Lt Col	HSU	129 & 104 GIAP	30 and 20 (plus 13 /4 in Spain)	451/112	
Bochkov, Ivan Vasil'evich	Capt	HSU	19 GIAP	8 and 32	350/50	4/4/43
Bogomazov, Grigorii Ivanovich	Sr Lt	HSU	103 GIAP	15 and 4 (some in other types)	400/60	
Bokii, Nikolai Andreevich	Sr Lt	HSU	2 GIAP-SF	17 and 1 (8 in P-39)	385/30	
Bondarenko, Vasilii Efimovich	Sr Lt	HSU	16 GIAP	24 (19 in P-39)	324/68	
Borisov, Ivan Grigor'evich	Sr Lt	HSU	9 GIAP	25 and 8	250/86	
Bukchin, S Z	Jr Lt		129 GIAP	12 and 2	116/37	
Burgunov, N F	Lt		129 GIAP	8	99/16	31/5/44
Burmatov, Vladimir Aleksandrovich	Sr Lt	HSU	255 IAP-SF	12 and 1	191/43	
Bychkov, Mikhail E	Lt		20 GIAP	6 and 7 (some in P-40)		23/9/43
Bykovets, Leonid Alekksandrovich	Sr Lt	HSU	28 GIAP	19 and 4	220/?	
Chapliev, Yu M	unknown		28 GIAP	9+		
Chepinoga, Pavel Yosifovich	Capt	HSU	213 GIAP	24 and 1 (some in Yak-1)	100+/?	
Chistov, Nikolai Aleksandrovich	Col		16 GIAP	19	300/?	
Chizh, Vasilii Ivanovich	Capt		69 GIAP	13	253/53	
Delegei, Nikolai Kupriyanovich	Lt Col	HSU	213 GIAP	15 and 3	200/30	
Devyataev, Mikhail Pavlovich	Sr Lt	HSU (in 1957)	104 GIAP	9 (possibly 6 in P-39)		PoW 13/7/44 Escaped from captivity
Didenko, Nikolai Matveevich	Sr Lt	HSU	2 GIAP-SF	15	378/50	
Dmitryuk, Grigorii Fedoseevich	Sr Lt	HSU	19 GIAP	18 (some in P-40) (also an ace in Korea)	206/37	
Dol'nikov, Grigorii Ustinovich	unknown	HSU	100 GIAP	15 and 1	160/42	
Doroshin, Vasilii Stepanovich	Capt		78 IAP-SF	8		23/6/43
Drygin, Nikolai Dmitrievich	Capt	HSU	104 GIAP	20 and 5 (2 in Yak-1?)	261+/40+	
Dzusov, Ibragim Magometovich	Maj Gen	HSU	100 GIAP	6 (also flew Yak-1 and P-40)	89/11	
Edkin, Viktor Dmitrievich	Maj	HSU	72 GIAP	15 and 3, + 2 balloons (7+ in Hurricane and Yak-7)		
Egorov, Aleksei Aleksandrovich	Capt	HSU	212 GIAP	24 and 7 (8 in Yak-7)	271/66	
Eliseev, Vladimir Stepanovich	unknown	HRF	67 GIAP	15 (6 in Hurricane and P-40)	256/70	
Elizarov, Sergei Mikhailovich	Sr Lt	HSU	9 GIAP	15 and 3	220/70	
Eryomin, Pavel Kuz'mich	Capt		16 GIAP	22		
Fadeev, Vadim Ivanovich	Capt	HSU	16 GIAP	18 and 3 (6 /1 in P-40 and Yak-1)	400/50	5/5/43
Fedorchuk, Igor Aleksandrovich	Lt	HSU	67 GIAP	15 (some in P-40)	136/70	
Figichev, Valentin Alekseevich	Maj	HSU	129 & 16 GIAP	21 (some in MiG and Yak-1)	621/?	
Filatov, Aleksandr Petrovich	Capt		30 GIAP	21 and 4	175/35	

Name	Rank	Award	Unit	Victories (Individual/shared)	sorties/combats	KIA
Filatov, A P	Sr Lt		67 GIAP	5+		20/4/45
Fomchenkov, Konstantin Fyodorovich	Capt	HSU	19 GIAP	9 and 26 (some in LaGG)		24/2/44
Fyodorov, Arkadii Vasilievich	Capt	HSU	16 GIAP	24 and 18 (some in other aircraft)	554/183	
Gaidaenko, Ivan Dmitrievich	Capt		19 GIAP	7 and 23		
Glinka, Boris Borisovich	Maj	HSU	100 GIAP	30	200+/?	
Glinka, Dmitrii Borisovich	Maj	2 x HSU	100 GIAP	50	300+/90	
Glotov, Nikolai Ivanovich	Sr Lt	HSU	129 GIAP	16 and 8	203/33	
Golovachyov, Pavel Yakovlevich	Capt	2 x HSU	9 GIAP	31 and 1 (many in LaGG, Yak and La-7)	457/125	
Golubev, Georgii Gordeevich	Sr Lt	HSU	16 GIAP	12	252/56	
Golushkov	Lt		21 GIAP	11		
Goreglyad, Leonid Ivanovich	Lt Col	HSU	22 GIAD	15 and 6	132/53	
Grachyov, Ivan Petrovich	Maj	HSU	28 & 68 GIAP	18 and 8 (7/4 in P-39) (1 taran)	203/94	14/9/44
Grafin, Iosif Ignatievich	Sr Lt		104 GIAP	19	200/?	28/2/45
Guchyok, Pyotr Iosifovich	Sr Lt	HSU	100 GIAP	18 and 3	209/56	18/4/45
Gulaev, Nikolai Dmitrievich	Maj	2 x HSU	129 GIAP	57 and 3 (4 tarans) (32 including 2 tarans in P-39)	248/69	
Ibatullin, Khasan Mingeevich	Lt Col		30 GIAP	15 (maybe 12 in P-39)	456/?	
Iskrin, Nikolai Mikhailovich	Sr Lt	HSU	16 GIAP	16 and 1 (6 in P-39)	297/80	
Kamozin, Pavel Mikhailovich	Capt	2 x HSU	66 & 101 GIAP	35 and 13 (at least 23/6 in P-39)	200/70	
Karasyov, Aleksandr Nikitovich	Sr Lt	HSU	9 GIAP	30 and 11 (14/9 in Yak-1) (7 victories in Korea)	380/112	PoW 7/4/44
Karlov, Valentin Andreevich	Sr Lt	HSU	129 GIAP	18 and 4	172/44	
Karmin, Aleksandr Leont'evich	Capt		129 GIAP	19 and 14 (1 taran)	221/31	
Kharlamov, M I	unknown		255 IAP-SF	7		
Kislyakov, Anatolii Vasil'evich	Capt	HSU	28 GIAP	15 and 1 balloon (most kills in P-39)	352/?	
Klimov, Pavel Dmitrievich	Jr Lt	HSU	2 GIAP- SF	11 and 16 (some in Hurricane)	306/33	
Klubov, Aleksandr Fyodorovich	Capt	2 x HSU	16 GIAP	31 and 19 (150 missions and 4 kills in I-153)	457/95	1/11/44
Kolomiets, Pyotr Leont'evich	Capt	HSU	2 GIAP-SF	18	400/?	
Kolyadin, Viktor Stepanovich	Sr Lt	HSU	68 GIAP	21	335/? (+ 350 as bomber pilot)	
Komel'kov, Mikhail Sergeevich	Maj	HSU	104 GIAP	32 and 7	321/75	
Konev, Georgii Nikolaevich	Lt Col	HSU	21 GIAP	17 and 18	313/98	30/12/42
Korolyov, Ivan Georgievich	Lt Col	HSU	9 GIAP	18 and 11 (some in other types)	500+/?	
Kotlov, Nikolai Stepanovich	Sr Lt		55 GIAP	17 and 3	253/?	2/6/43
Kovachevich, Arkadii Fyodorovich	Capt	HSU	9 GIAP	26 and 6 (13 in P-39)	520/?	
Koval, Dmitrii Ivanovich	Lt	HSU	45 IAP	10 and 3 or 13 and 3 (some in Yak-1)	150/30	8/5/43
Kozhevnikov, Anatolii Leonidovich	Maj	HSU	212 GIAP	27 (11 in Hurricane and Yak)	300/69	
Krivosheev, Efim Avtonomovich	Lt	HSU	19 GIAP	7 and 15 (1 taran)	97/30	9/9/42
Kryukov, Pavel Pavlovich	Lt Col	HSU	16 GIAP	19 and 1 (perhaps 10 in P-39)	650/?	
Kudrya, I	Sgt		45 IAP	6		
Kudrya, Nikolai Danilovich	Jr Lt	HSU	45 IAP	11	53/24	26/5/43
Kukharenko, Andrei Nikitovich	Col		2 GIAP-SF	15 (some in other types)	300+/?	
Kutakhov, Pavel Stepanovich	Col	HSU	19 GIAP	13 and 28 (1 in I-16)	367/79	
Kuznetsov, Georgii Dmitrievich	Capt		16 GIAP	10 and 12	350/?	
Kuznetsov, Nikolai Fyodorovich	Maj	HSU	67 GIAP	36 and 12 (17 in P-39)	400/?	
Lagutenko, Ivan Nikitovich	Maj	HSU	68 GIAP	17 and 3 (some in other aircraft)	288/79	
Latyshev, Vladimir Aleksandrovich	Sr Lt	HSU	67 GIAP	17 (some in other aircraft)	232/?	

87

Name	Rank	Award	Unit	Victories (Individual/shared)	sorties/combats	KIA
Lavitskii, Nikolai Efimovich	Capt	HSU	100 GIAP	24 and 2 (11/1 in I-153 and Yak-1)	250/100	10/3/44
Lavrinenkov, Vladimir Dmitrievich	Maj	2 x HSU	9 GIAP	36 and 11 (22/11 in Yak-1, 3 in La-7)	448/134	
Likhobabin, Ivan Dmitrievich	Maj	HSU	72 GIAP	30 and 9	321/60	
Likhovid, Mikhail Stepanovich	Sr Lt	HSU	104 GIAP	16 and 11	204/44	12/8/44
Limarenko, Vasilii Alekseevich	Capt		54 GIAP	15 and 7 (perhaps 5 in P-39)	300	
Litvinchuk, Boris Mikhailovich	Capt	HSU	11 GIAP-ChF	15 or 18	459/44	
Logvinov, I I	unknown		28 GIAP	14		
Lukíyanov, Sergei Ivanovich	Lt Col	HSU	16 GIAP	19 and 15 (2 in I-16)	356/?	
Lusto, Mikhail Vasil'evich	Sr Lt	HSU	129 GIAP	18 and 1	169/36	
Makarenko, Nikolai Fyodorovich	Maj	HSU	153 IAP	10 (9 in P-39)	320/?	
Mariinskii, Evgenii Pakhomovich	Sr Lt	HSU	129 GIAP	21	200/60	
Maslov, V	Jr Lt		101 GIAP	5	115/?	
Mazurin, Fyodor Mikhailovich	Capt	HSU	28 GIAP	19 and 2	222/50	
Mikhailik, Yakov Danilovich	Sr Lt	HSU	54 GIAP	17 and 6 (5 in P-39)	316/73	
Mikhalyov, Vasilii Pavlovich	Sr Lt	HSU	213 GIAP	22 and 4 (2 tarans in a single sortie)		
Mironov, Viktor Petrovich	Capt	HSU	19 GIAP	10 and 15 (5 and 15 in P-39)	356/?	16/2/43
Mozutko, N T	Lt		438 IAP	5	108/38	1/6/44
Narzhimskii, Vladimir Aleksandrovich	Capt	HSU	11 GIAP-ChF	18 and 5 (most in P-39)	404/40+	
Nikiforov, Pyotr Pavlovich	Capt	HSU	129 GIAP	20 and 4	297/69	
Nikitin, Aleksei Ivanovich	Lt	HSU	28 GIAP	19 and 5 (10 in P-39)	238/73	
Novichkov, Stepan Matveevich	Lt Col	HSU	67 GIAP	29 (19 in P-40)	315/?	
Novikov, Aleksei Ivanovich	Capt	HSU	17 IAP	22 (some in other types)	500/?	
Obraztsov, Yurii	unknown		100 GIAP	10+		
Olifirenko, I K	Capt		16 GIAP	14		10/5/44
Orlov, M I	Sr Lt		213 GIAP	6 and 3	60/19	
Orlov, Pavel Ivanovich	Capt	HSU	2 GIAP-SF	11 (at least 4 in other types)	276/24	15/3/43
Panin, Pavel Alekseevich	Maj	HSU	255 IAP-SF	13 (some in LaGG)	114/18	26/8/43
Pankratov, Sergei Stepanovich	Maj	HSU	66 IAP	19 and 9	264/52	
Pasechnik	Capt		30 GIAP	15+		
Pas'ko, Nikolai Fyodorovich	Sr Lt	HSU	28 GIAP	15 and 1 balloon	265/32	
Petrenko, Evgenii Vasil'evich	Capt	HSU	20 IAP-SF	15 and 1 (some in Yak)	293/75	
Petrov, Mikhail Georgievich	unknown	HRF	100 GIAP	15 and 1	352/80	
Piskunov, Ivan	Sgt		72 GIAP	12		
Pokhlebaev, Ivan Grigor'evich	Sr Lt	HSU	101 GIAP	20	138/42	
Pokryshkin, Aleksandr Ivanovich	Lt Col	3 x HSU	16 GIAP	59 and 6	650+/156	
Proshenkov, Nikolai Ivanovich	Maj	HSU	69 GIAP	19 and 4	375/86	
Rassadkin, Pyotr Alekseevich	Capt	HSU	255 IAP-SF	12	190/?	
Razumov, Ivan Ivanovich	Jr Lt		20 GIAP	7	198/?	
Rechkalov, Grigorii Andreevich	Capt	2 x HSU	16 GIAP	56 and 6 (52/4 in P-39)	450/122	
Rents, Mikhail Petrovich	Maj	HSU	30 GIAP	20 and 5	261/63	
Rudenko, Anatolii Vladimirovich	unknown		28 IAP	14 (some in other aircraft)	350/?	
Sakharov, Pavel Ivanovich	Capt	HSU	78 IAP-SF	9	157/18	
Savin, Ivan	unknown		16 GIAP	6+		
Semenishin, Vladimir Grigor'evich	Lt Col	HSU	104 GIAP	23 and 13 (perhaps some in I-16)	300/	29/2/43
Sergov, Aleksei Ivanovich	Maj	HSU	213 GIAP	17 and 17	500/?	
Sgibnev, Pyotr Georgievich	Capt	HSU	78 IAP-SF	19 (16 in Hurricane)	318/38	5/3/43
Sharenko, Vasilii Denisovich	Maj	HSU	100 GIAP	16 and 4	300/70	30/7/44
Shcherbakov, Viktor Ivanovich	Sr Lt	HSU	11 GIAP-ChF	11 and 7	359/35	
Shevelyov, Pavel Fyodorovich	Capt	HSU	67 GIAP	17 and 2 (some in P-40) (3 kills in Korea)	258/78	
Shikunov, F I	Lt		9 GIAP	25 (some in other types)		
Shipov, Aleksandr Pavlovich	Capt	HSU	20 IAP-SF	11	68/21	

Name	Rank	Award	Unit	Victories (Individual/shared)	sorties/combats	KIA
Shishkin, Vasilii Ivanovich	Maj	HSU	55 GIAP	15 and 16 (majority in Yak)	520/78	
Sirotin, Vyacheslav Fyodorovich	Maj	HSU	17 IAP	26	300/?	
Smirnov, Aleksei Semyonovich	Maj	2 x HSU	28 GIAP	34 and 1 (4 in I-153)	457/?	
Snesaryov, Vladimir Semyonovich	Capt	HSU	11 GIAP-ChF	16 and 8	314/40	
Sobolev, Nikolai Grigor'evich	Lt Col		21 GIAP	17+ (some in LaGG?)		
Sokolov, V V	Maj		438 IAP	12	129/34	31/5/44
Sopin, A I	Jr Lt		438 IAP	5	122/32	
Starchikov, Nikolai Aleekseevich	Capt	HSU	16 GIAP	18 and 1	489/89	
Starikov, Dmitrii Aleksandrovich	Sr Lt	HSU	11 GIAP-ChF	21 and 6 (9 in Yak)	479/51	
Strelínikov, Vasilii Polikarpovich	Capt	HSU	78 IAP-SF	6	150/14	
Stroikov, Nikolai Vasil'evich	Sr Lt	HSU	213 GIAP	14 and 21	245/66	
Sukhov, Konstantin Vasil'evich	Sr Lt	HSU	16 GIAP	22 (3 in I-153 and I-16)	350/57	
Svinarenko, Ivan Lukich	Capt		100 GIAP	10 and 6		
Svistunov, Anatolii Ivanovich	Capt	HSU	213 GIAP	14 and 21	274/68	
Taranenko, Ivan Andreevich	Lt Col	HSU	104 GIAP	16 and 4 (4/4 in P-39)	265/50	
Tarasov, Aleksei Kondrat'evich	Capt	HSU	20 IAP-SF	10 (some in Yak)	213/48	
Tarasov, Ivan	unknown		9 GIAP	19 (in Yak-1, P-39 and La-7)		
Tashchiev, Suren	Capt		11 GIAP-ChF	11	400/?	25/9/43
Trofimov, Nikolai Leont'evich	Capt	HSU	16 GIAP	15 and 11	341/72	
Trud, Andrei Ivanovich	Lt	HSU	16 GIAP	24 and 1	600/71+	
Tsvetkov, Veniamin P	Capt		16 GIAP	14	420/130	2/45
Tvelenev, Mikhail Stepanovich	Capt	HSU	9 GIAP	18 and 28 (some in Yak-1 and La-7)	420/130	
Uglanskii, Pyotr	Sr Lt		28 GIAP	14		
Vilíyamson, Aleksandr Aleksandrovich	Capt	HSU	104 GIAP	18 and 6 (some in I-16 and Yak-1)	382/66	
Vinogradov, Aleksei Aleksandrovich	Jr Lt		30 GIAP	10	115/19	
Vishnevitskii, Konstantin Grigor'evich	Maj	HSU	104 GIAP	20 and 15 (some in I-16 and Yak-1)	200/?	30/7/44
Zadirako, L V	Lt		129 GIAP	5 and 1	54/37	
Zakalyuk, Aleksei Semyonovich	Capt		104 GIAP	16	594/90	
Zavarukhin, Pavel Filippovich	Lt Col		72 GIAP	13 and 4	480/?	
Zharikov, Ivan Mikhailovich	Capt		20 GIAP	9 and 16 (some in P-40)	300/?	
Zherdev, Viktor Ivanovich	Capt		16 GIAP	12	131/45	
Zhuchenko, Ivan Yakovlevich	Sr Lt		20 GIAP	11		
Ziborov, Vasilii Mikhailovich	Sr Lt	HSU	72 GIAP	22	180/38	
Zyuzin, Dmitrii Vasil'evich	Sr Lt	HSU	11 GIAP-ChF	15	535+/51+	

APPENDIX V

Serials and Bort Numbers of aircraft flown by Soviet Aces

Bochkov, Ivan Vasil'evich	Airacobra Is AH962 #12, AH726 #36 and BX168 #15
Gaidaenko, Ivan Dmitrievich	Airacobra Is AH660 and AH636 #33
Krivosheev, Efim Avtonomovich	Airacobra I BX320 #16
Pas'ko, Nikolai Fyodorovich	Airacobra I BX254
Babak, Ivan Il'ich	P-39D-2 41-38416 and P-39N-0 42-9033 #01
Dol'nikov, Grigorii Ustinovich	P-39N-0 42-9033 #01
Drygin, Nikolai Dmitrievich	P-39D-2 41-38421
Glinka, Boris Borisovich	P-39D-2 41-38431
Glinka, Dmitrii Boriovich	P-39K-1 42- 4403 #21
Fadeev, Vadim Ivanovich	P-39D-2 41-38428 #37
Iskrin, Nikolai Mikhailovich	P-39D-2 41-38555 #27
Likhovid, Mikhail Stepanovich	P-39D-2 41-38455
Petrov, Mikhail Georgievich	P-39K-1 42-4606
Pokryshkin, Aleksandr Ivanovich	P-39D-2 41-38520 #13 and P-39N-0 42-9004 #100

Rechkalov, Grigorii Andreevich	P-39D-2 41-38547 #40, P-39N-0 42-8747 and P-39Q-15 44-2547 #RGA
Zakalyuk, Aleksei Semyonovich	P-39D-2 41-38457
Klubov, Aleksandr Fyodorovich	P-39N-1 42-9434 #45 and P-39N-1 42-9589 #125
Bilyukhin, Aleksandr Dmitrievich	#53
Filatov, Aleksandr Petrovich	P-39Q-5 42-20414 #93 Yellow
Golubev, Georgii Gordeevich	#19
Ibatullin, Khasan Mingeevich	P-39N-1 42-9625
Orlov, M I	P-39Q-15 44-2823
Rents, Mikhail Petrovich	P-39N-1 42-9553 #84
Stroikov, N V	P-39Q-25 44-32286 #77
Sukhov, Konstantin Vasil'evich	P-39N #50
Zadirako, L V	P-39N-5 42-18662

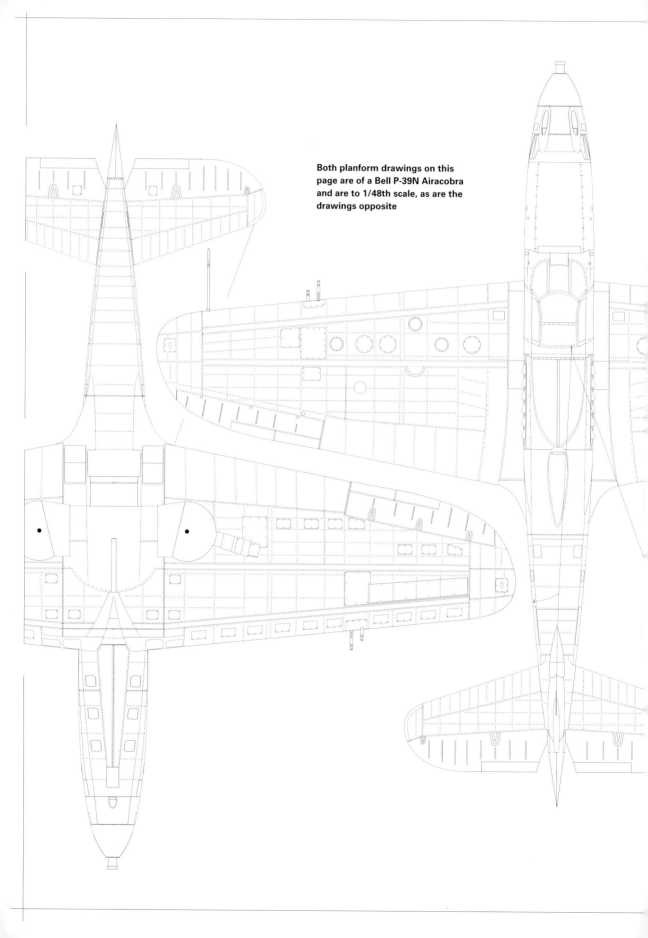

Both planform drawings on this page are of a Bell P-39N Airacobra and are to 1/48th scale, as are the drawings opposite

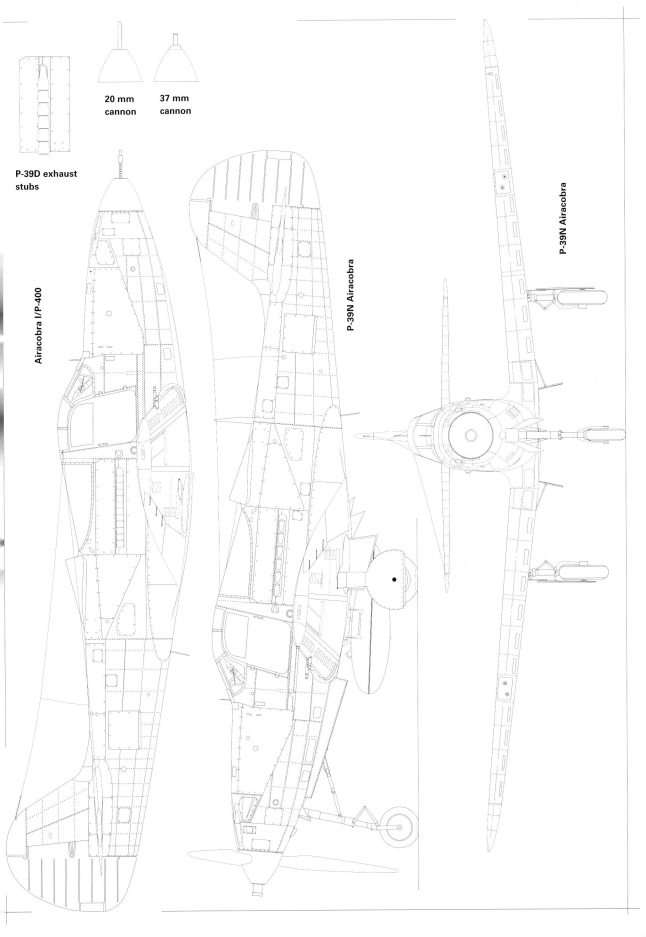

P-39D exhaust stubs

20 mm cannon

37 mm cannon

Airacobra I/P-400

P-39N Airacobra

P-39N Airacobra

COLOUR PLATES

1

P-400 BW146 *Whistlin' Britches* of Lt Zed Fountain, 67th FS, Tontouta, New Caledonia, May 1942

Fountain trained on this aircraft in New Caledonia prior to the 67th FS being thrown into action from Henderson Field, on Guadalcanal. He was part of 'Patsy Flight', which first used the sharksmouth motif that would eventually adorn most 67th FS fighters. Squadron records credit Fountain with as many as 5.5 victories, although officially he was awarded just a single kill for a Japanese floatplane shot down on 3 December 1942.

2

P-39F 41-7116 of Lt Grover Gholson, 36th FS/8th FG, Port Moresby, New Guinea, May 1942

This P-39 was the first of 229 F-models to roll off Bell's Buffalo, New York, production line in early 1942 – this version differed from the preceding D-model by employing a 10 ft 4 in diameter Aeroproducts propeller in place of the Curtiss-Electric prop. 41-7116 was almost certainly issued to the 36th FS just prior to the unit's move to New Guinea. Gholson does not remember much about this particular P-39, for most engagements fought in the vicinity of Port Moresby during this period saw pilots hastily strapping into any available fighter on the flightline once ordered to scramble. What he does remember, however, is that the P-39 was in clean condition, and free of unit markings except for the pre-war U.S. ARMY titling beneath the wings.

3

P-400 (serial unknown) *Wahl Eye II/"PAT"* of Lt Eugene Wahl, 39th FS/35th FG, Port Moresby, New Guinea, May 1942

Lt Wahl scored one of the 39th FS's first victories on 26 May 1942 when he downed a Zero near Mt Lawson, north of Port Moresby – the fighter was seen to crash by observers on the ground. Future 20-kill ace Tom Lynch scored his third P-39 victory during the same engagement, and Frank Adkins claimed his only P-39 kill to add to the two Zeros he had destroyed in Java the previous February whilst flying P-40Es with the 17th PS. The latter pilot would 'make ace' by downing two Bf 109s over Germany in August 1944, Adkins serving as CO of the P-47-equipped 313th FS/50th FG at the time. The sharksmouth on Wahl's P-400 was a personal marking, and was in no way associated with the 'teeth' that subsequently adorned the 39th FS's P-38s in 1943. Note that the fighter has had the red centre to its national marking deleted, this being painted out from May onwards in order to avoid any confusion with the Japanese 'meatball'. The 8th FG was far too occupied in battle to have the markings on its Airacobras altered in conformity with the new practice, so the old red-centred star was used up until its two squadrons were relieved in June. The change was eventually made in Australia in July through the simple 'field application' of a coat of white paint.

4

P-400 BW176 of Lt Charles King, 39th FS/35th FG, Port Moresby, New Guinea, June 1942

One pilot who appreciated the good points of the P-39, even if he did subsequently score all five of his victories in the P-38,

was Charlie King. He flew this P-400 throughout his first combat tour in mid-1942, BW176 then being transferred to the 80th FS when the unit relieved the 39th late in July. The veteran fighter remained on operations until at least January 1943.

5

P-400 BW102 *THE FLAMING* (Arrow) of Lt Curran 'Jack' Jones, 39th FS/35th FG, Port Moresby, New Guinea, June 1942

Future five-kill ace 'Jack' Jones is known to have regularly flown this P-400 during the 39th's first tour of operations in mid-1942. Indeed, he may well have used it to claim his sole Airacobra kill (a Zero) on the morning of 9 June. Like most other P-400s from the 39th FS, BW102 was transferred to the 80th FS sometime in July 1942. Its new owners removed the arrow motif and added a large sharksmouth and eyes in its place. The fighter was also adorned with the identification letter 'K' forward of the cockpit door.

6

P-39D-1 41-38338 *Nip's Nemesis II* of Lt Don C McGee, 36th FS/8th FG, Port Moresby, New Guinea, June 1942

One of the few P-39 pilots to have more than one victory confirmed during the 8th FG's initial combat deployment to New Guinea, 'Fibber' McGee still maintains that he downed at least five aircraft with the Airacobra in 1942. One of those unconfirmed kills was officially recorded as a probable (a Zero attacked on 5 May near Port Moresby), whilst another unspecified engagement saw McGee credited with having at least damaged one Japanese aircraft. In any event, his single Zero kill on 1 May, followed by a pair of Mitsubishi fighters 28 days later, were officially recognised. It remains unclear whether McGee scored any of his victories with this particular P-39, which was assigned to him after *Nip's Nemesis* (I) was damaged beyond repair during the engagement of 1 May.

7

P-39J 41-7073 of Lt Leslie Spoonts, 57th FS/54th FG, Kodiak, Alaska, June-October 1942

The 57th FS was sent on emergency temporary duty to the Aleutians during the Japanese invasion in June 1942, the unit being stationed on Kodiak Island from mid-942 until it returned to Bartow Field, Florida, in early 1943. Leslie Spoonts apparently believed that he had destroyed at least three Japanese aircraft during his combat tour, although these were almost certainly claimed after strafing attacks on floatplanes found in the waters surrounding the Japanese-held islands – there are no official records crediting Spoonts with any aerial kills. The P-39Q-20 (44-3908) on display in the USAF Museum in Dayton, Ohio, is painted in the markings of Spoonts' J-model. The original 41-7073 was one of only 25 P-39Js built, this version differing from late-build F-models through the fitment of an improved V-1710-59 (E12) engine that boasted an automatic manifold pressure regulator.

8

P-39D (serial unknown) of Lt Joseph McKeon, 35th FS/ 8th FG, Milne Bay, New Guinea, November 1942

Joe McKeon destroyed a Zero over Buna on 7 December 1942 whilst flying P-39D-1 41-38353, this victory being his sole success with the Bell fighter. The Airacobra illustrated here was assigned to him earlier in the year, and was apparently damaged or destroyed in a landing accident in November. McKeon transferred to the 475th FG's 433rd FS during the summer of 1943, and scored four victories flying P-38s in September-October of that same year. Having completed 155 combat missions in the Pacific, McKeon briefly returned home, before volunteering for service in the ETO with the 20th FG's 77th FS. He duly claimed a Bf 109 destroyed and an Fw 190 damaged in August 1944, and had completed 40 missions in P-38s and P-51s when he was forced to abandon his Mustang following a collision over Germany on 7 October. Bailing out, McKeon was quickly captured, and he spent the rest of the war as a PoW.

9

P-39D-1 41-36345 *Pelikia* of Lt George Welch, 36th FS/ 8th FG, Milne Bay, New Guinea, November 1942

'Wheaties' Welch was also involved in the 36th FS's legendary Buna engagement on 7 December 1942, the Pearl Harbor veteran adding no fewer than four victories (two Zeros and two 'Vals') to the quartet of kills he had claimed exactly one year earlier. As with Joe McKeon's profiled P-39, this particular machine was apparently used by Welch before the December 1942 engagement over Buna (he was flying P-39D-1 41-38359 on this occasion), and had also been either written off or at least damaged in a heavy landing during November.

10

P-39D-1 41-38295 of Lt Gerald R Johnson, 57th FS/54th FG, Kodiak, Alaska, late 1942

Future 22-kill ace 'Jerry' Johnson was just as eager with the P-39 as he would later prove to be in action with the P-38 over the Southwest Pacific. He engaged A6M2N 'Rufe' floatplane fighters in the Kiska-Adak area on 25 September and 1 October 1942, and months later was awarded two probable kills by the Fifth Air Force (his controlling body in the Pacific), but not by the Eleventh Air Force, which ran the air war in the Aleutians! It denied these claims on the grounds that there was no eyewitness evidence of either fighter crashing into the sea.

11

P-39K-1 42-4358 of Lt William McDonough, 40th FS/ 35th FG, Nadzab, New Guinea, February 1943

McDonough's flight adorned its P-39s with elaborate nose-art in the form of Disney cartoon characters, 42-4358 being decorated with a belligerent 'Donald Duck' on the starboard side – the fighters carried the artwork on this side only. Other characters featured included Walt Disney's 'Goofy' and Warner Brothers 'Bugs Bunny'. Future five-kill ace McDonough claimed two Zeros with 42-4358 on 2 February 1943 over Wau.

12

P-39N (serial unknown) of Lt William K Giroux, 32nd FS/ 52nd FG, Panama Canal Zone, April 1943

'Kenny' Giroux flew this P-39N during his uneventful tour of duty defending the Panama Canal Zone in 1943. No aerial engagements occurred in the Caribbean during World War 2, and fighter pilots were left to perform mundane coastal patrols or convoy escort, giving pilots assigned to the Canal Zone area little chance of gaining operational experience. The only identifying mark worn by P-39s assigned to the 32nd FS was the patch of white paint applied to the fin tip, although Giroux

further personalised his fighter with the figure of a knight on the left door. Eager to see action, Giroux was posted to the 8th FG's 36th FS in late 1943, and duly claimed ten Japanese aircraft destroyed flying the P-38 in 1944 – eight of these were downed in the first two weeks of November alone!

13

P-39D-2 41-38506 of Lt Lloyd 'Yogi' Rosser, 41st FS/ 35th FG, Port Moresby, New Guinea, April-June 1943

'Yogi' Rosser scored his solitary kill on 12 April 1943, when he downed a 'Betty' that was part of a large formation sent to attack Port Moresby. Both of the 35th FG's P-39 squadrons engaged the enemy on this day, and were credited with destroying 12 of the 28 aircraft reportedly shot down. The remaining kills marked on this fighter were almost certainly claimed by other pilots that flew 41-38506 during this period.

14

P-39L-1 42-4520 *"EVELYN"* of Lt Hugh Dow, 346th FS/ 350th FG, Maison Blanche, Algeria, Spring 1943

Although Hugh Dow was photographed sitting in this particular machine, his regular mount was marked with the identification letter 'D' on the cockpit door, and carried the name *Rowdy* (the pilot's nickname). It may have been that Dow had simply flown 'V' on the day that someone thought it significant to photograph 42-4520 due to its identification letter symbolising the Allied victory symbol in World War 2. In any event, this machine was representative of most P-39s that fought in North Africa, as it sports both the 346th FS's single letter marking and the 81st FG's 'X-R' codes.

15

P-39N (serial unknown) of Lt Bill Fiedler, 68th and 70th FSs/347th FG, Guadalcanal, circa June 1943

The USAAF's sole Airacobra-only ace, Bill Fiedler served with both the 68th and 70th FSs during his combat tour in the Pacific in 1943. He was certainly as aggressive as anyone in those redoubtable squadrons, and possessed sufficient skill (and luck) to claim three Zeros and two 'Vals' destroyed between January and June 1943. His luck ran out, however, on 30 June when his P-39 was struck by a P-38 that was taking off from Guadalcanal. He had been sitting on the wing of his idling fighter at the end of the runway, waiting his turn to take off, when one of the departing Lightnings suffered a loss of power and crashed into the clutch of stationary P-39s, killing Fiedler.

16

P-39 (unknown sub-type and serial) of Lt Bob Yaeger, 40th FS/35th FG, Tsili-Tsili, New Guinea, August 1943

Yaeger claimed a 'Lily' and an 'Oscar' in this P-39 on 15 August 1943 in the Tsili-Tsili area. Within weeks of this action having taken place, the 40th FS had commenced its conversion onto the Thunderbolt. Yaeger would 'make ace' in the P-47 on 11 March 1944 when he destroyed two 'Tonys' and an 'Oscar'.

17

P-39 (unknown sub-type and serial) of Capt Tom Winburn, 40th FS/35th FG, Tsili-Tsili, New Guinea, August 1943

Winburn claimed two Zeros destroyed (his only kills) during the 40th FS's memorable engagement of 6 February 1943, and as this aircraft was his regular mount, he may have used it on this day. He was made CO of the 40th FS on 25 April, and remained in command until ending his tour in early November.

18

P-39N-5 42-18805 *TODDY III* of Capt Hilbert, 41st FS/ 35th FG, Tsili-Tsili, New Guinea, September 1943

The first N-models entered service with the 41st FS in April 1943, and this particular example was issued to a Capt Hilbert (christian name unknown), who was a flight leader with the unit during its most productive spell with the P-39 – between April and September 1943, when the 41st claimed 18 kills.

19

P-39L-1 42-4687 *Little Toni*, flown by various pilots of the 362nd FS/357th FG, Hayward, California, September 1943

Future ETO aces such as 'Chuck' Yeager and 'Bud' Anderson were impressed with the P-39, these tyro fighter pilots flying many hours in aircraft such as this one during the 357th FG's pre-deployment training in California in 1943. Both individuals commented that the P-39 was a pleasure to fly – providing that you engaged in aerial combat in another type of fighter!

20

P-39N-5 43-18802 of Lt Roy Owen, 41st FS/35th FG, Nadzab, New Guinea, October 1943

The 41st FS had scored 92 aerial victories by the end of World War 2, although the solitary claim made by the pilot of this lavishly decorated machine, Roy Owen, was not one of them. He is listed within squadron reports as having lodged one unspecified claim, which was almost certainly reduced to a probable or damaged by the victory assessment board.

21

P-39Q-10 42-20746 *OLD CROW* of Lt 'Bud' Anderson, 363rd FS/357th FG, Oroville, California, October 1943

This particular aircraft was the very first fighter assigned to future high-scoring ace 'Bud' Anderson. He quickly dubbed it *OLD CROW*, and this name was to appear on all future fighters flown by him, ranging from the P-51 Mustang through to the F-105 Thunderchief. One of the first pilots transferred into the newly-formed 357th FG, Anderson, like his squadronmate and close friend 'Chuck' Yeager, appreciated the P-39 as a trainer, but much preferred the P-51 for actual combat. All three squadrons within the group flew Airacobras from a series of bases in California and Nevada prior to shipping out for the ETO in November 1943. Once in Britain the 357th received P-51Bs.

22

P-39N-1 42-18409 of Lt Harold Nus, 41st FS/35th FG, Nadzab, New Guinea, November 1943

This particular P-39 was one of the last to see service with the 41st FS prior to the unit re-equipping with the P-47 in January 1944. Squadron records indicate that Nus used it to shoot down a Ki-48 'Lily' bomber (his sole kill) near Tsili-Tsili during the 41st's high-scoring action of 15 August 1943.

23

P-39Q-1 42-19510 *SAD SACK* of Capt James Van Nada, 72nd FS, Guadalcanal, December 1943

Van Nada participated in one of the few engagements experienced by Seventh Air Force P-39 pilots when he teamed up with a squadronmate to down a G4M 'Betty' bomber on 27 December 1943. He would later assume command of the 72nd FS prior to ending his tour.

24

Airacobra I AH636 'White 33' of Capt Ivan Dmitrievich Gaidaenko, 19 GIAP, Autumn 1942

All Airacobra Is received from the UK by the USSR were finished in the standard RAF camouflage of Dark Green and Ocean Grey upper surfaces, and Medium Sea Grey lower surfaces. Gaidaenko's *Kobra* has four red victory stars for individual kills and 20 white outline stars representing shared victories. 19 GIAP placed its aircraft identification (Bort) number on the tail fin of its aircraft. AH636 was Gaidaenko's second *Kobra*, for he had previously been shot down in AH660.

25

P-39D-2 41-38428 'White 37' of Capt Vadim Ivanovich Fadeev, 16 GIAP, April 1943

At the time of his death, Vadim Fadeev was one of 16 GIAP's leading pilots, with 18 individual and 3 shared victories. Like all P-39s received via lend-lease from the USA, it was finished in the standard USAAF finish of Olive Drab uppersurfaces and Neutral Gray undersurfaces. During this early period, the Soviet red star (sometimes outlined in black) was painted directly over the American white star, with the the blue disc left in place. On such machines, red stars were placed both on the upper and lower wing surfaces on both wings, giving an asymmetric effect, for the original American stars were applied on the underside of one wing only. In 1943, when P-39s were arriving in small quantities, no time was taken to overpaint the original USAAF yellow serial numbers either. The red spinner and tip of the vertical fin on this machine were regular identifying marks used by 16 GIAP from the beginning of 1943 until the end of the war. Like most P-39 units, this regiment located its identification numbers on the rear fuselage of its aircraft.

26

P-39K-1 42-4403 'White 21' of Snr Lt Dmitrii Borisovich Glinka, 45 IAP, Kuban, Spring 1943

A twice HSU winner, Dmitrii Glinka finished the war with 50 victories to his name. Thanks to his exploits, and numerous others within the regiment, 45 IAP was awarded Guards status and redesignated 100 GIAP in August 1943. His P-39 is marked with the red fin tip and spinner synonymous with fighters controlled by 216 SAD/9 GIAD. By mid-1943 the fighter's stars had swapped their black outlines for a white border.

27

P-39Q (serial unknown) 'White 10' of Capt Pavel Stepanovich Kutakhov, 19 GIAP, Shongui, late 1943

Pavel Kutakhov ended the war as a colonel, with 13 individual and 28 shared victories to his name. Post-war, he became the commander of the Soviet Air Forces. This late-build P-39 has had the American insignias and serial numbers overpainted with green paint soon after its arrival in the Soviet Union. On such aircraft, there were generally no stars on the upper surfaces of the wings. Kutakhov's machine also features a non-standard red nose, which was possibly used to identify its pilot as a squadron commander. It has 8 red victory stars and 13 outline stars, representing his individual and shared victories.

28

P-39N 'Silver 24' (serial and pilot unknown), 191 IAP, Leningrad Front, Summer 1944

191 IAP was assigned to the Leningrad Air Defence Zone, and saw combat over southern Finland in 1944. This regiment was one of those which placed Bort numbers on the nose ahead of the cockpit, instead of on the rear fuselage. It was also notable for using silver, or aluminum, paint instead of white both for its unit numbers and for outlining the national marking – rudders and the spinners were also frequently painted metallic.

29

P-39Q-25 44-32286 'White 77' of Sr Lt Nikolai Vasil'evich Stroikov, 213 GIAP, Poland, September 1944

Nikolai Stroikov, who flew with 213 GIAP's 2nd squadron, scored 14 individual and 21 shared victories. This aircraft features typical camouflage and markings for a P-39 in 1944, with the significant addition of a red outline to the star's white border. Note the ten solid red and three red and white victory stars, distinguishing between Stroikov's individual and shared kills. The wide white diagonal band on the tail is a formation marking, which was introduced into the VVS from mid-1944.

30

P-39N-1 42-9434 'White 45' of Capt Aleksandr Fyodorovich Klubov, 16 GIAP, Poland, October 1944

Aleksandr Klubov scored 31 individual and 19 shared victories, and received his second HSU posthumously after he was killed in a flying accident. This machine has the typical finish for a P-39 of 16 GIAP, with Klubov's victory stars on the nose. Again, the white stars signify his shared kills.

31

P-39Q-5 42-20414 'Yellow 93' of Capt Aleksandr Filatov, 30 GIAP, Poland, Autumn 1944

Aleksandr Filatov flew this P-39Q-5 from early 1944, and like all American-supplied Airacobras, it was finished in standard Olive Drab and Neutral Gray. The spinner and tip of the tail fin were painted blue, which denoted either the fighter's regiment or squadron. Bort number 'Yellow 93' was displayed on the aircraft's nose, as was common practice within P-39 units. Soviet aviators' wings were painted on both cockpit doors, and this marking seems to have been adopted as a regimental badge. Filatov had his victory tally applied on the left side of the fuselage between the rear cockpit transparency and the exhaust stubs. Most dramatic of the myriad markings worn on this fighter was Filatov's individual insignia – a poker hand of three cards, the Ace, Seven and Queen of Spades. This marking was inspired both by the card game and Pushkin's famous story 'Queen of Spades', and it signified Filatov's love of literature and poetry. Some might note that the hand on the ace's aircraft totals 20 – on 19 April 1945 he scored his 21st victory, and on 20 April, when he tried to exceed '21', he 'went bust'.

32 & 33

P-39N-0 42-9033 'White 01' of Capt Ivan Il'ich Babak, 100 GIAP, Germany, January 1945

Ivan Babak scored 33 individual and 4 shared victories, and would have received a second HSU except for the fact that he was shot down and captured on 22 April 1945. Issued with this aircraft in September 1943, Babak's P-39 has a white fin tip, denoting its assignment to 9 GIAD's 100 GIAP. The inscription beneath the cockpit reads *From the schoolchildren of Mariupol*, disregarding the fact that all lend-lease P-39s sent to the USSR were paid for by American taxpayers, rather than Russian contributions – the inscription might more appropriately have gone on a Yak or Lavochkin! Finally, Babak adorned the right hand side of his fighter with a sword- and trumpet-wielding angel. When the ace transferred to 16 GIAP, this veteran aircraft was passed to Grigorii Dol'nikov, who had the markings partially changed (see profiles 36 and 37).

34

P-39N (serial unknown) 'White 50' of Sr Lt Konstantin Vasil'evich Sukhov, 16 IAP, Germany, February 1945

Konstantin Sukhov scored 22 victories, almost 30 years after the war became chief air advisor to the Syrian Air Force, taking part in the 1973 October War with Israel. This aircraft was photographed taking off from a German autobahn in the final weeks of the war. It has the usual camouflage, and regular red spinner and fin tip of 16 GIAP, but is unusual in retaining its transit markings with the white circles as a background for the red stars. In such circumstances, the stars would have also been applied in a similar fashion on the wing uppersurfaces.

35

P-39N-0 42-9004 'White 100' of Col Aleksandr Ivanovich Pokryshkin, 9 GIAD, Germany, Spring 1945

Three-time HSU, Aleksandr Pokryshkin, with 59 officially credited individual victories, was the second-ranking Allied ace of World War 2. While Bort '100' seems to have been the number used by commanders of several different regiments and divisions for their fighters, Pokryshkin had always marked his machines 'White 100' from his first days in action in 1941. Aside from the many victory stars and Bort number, this P-39 is marked as a typical Airacobra of 16 GIAP, and 9 GIAD. The significance of the white border to the red fin tip remains unclear, for it appeared on both division HQ and regiment aircraft.

36 & 37

P-39N-0 42-9033 'White 01'of Grigorii Ustinovich Dol'nikov, 100 GIAP, Germany May 1945.

When Ivan Babak was given command of 16 GIAP in February 1945, his aircraft was inherited by his friend and fellow ace Grigorii Dol'nikov. Naturally, he retained the dedication inscription, but dispensed with the personal markings of Babak. When ace Pyotr Guchyok was killed in action on 18 April 1945, Dol'nikov had the inscription *For Petya Guchyok* painted over the angel on the right side of the P-39. Four days later Ivan Babak was also downed and presumed killed, so Dol'nikov placed another inscription (*For Vanya Babak*) on the left side.

38

P-39N-1 42-9553 'White 84' of Maj Mikhail Rents, 30 GIAP, Germany, Spring 1945

Mikhail Rents flew this P-39N from the beginning of 1944 until war's end. It was painted much like Filatov's fighter, except that its Bort number was inexplicably applied in white instead of yellow. On the left fuselage, to the rear of the cockpit, Rents had the motto *za pogibshikh brat'ev* ('for my perished brothers') applied, this slogan honouring his two brothers who had died at the front, and a third who had returned home legless.

INDEX

References to illustrations are shown in **bold**. Plates are shown with page and caption locators in brackets.